CU00841480

3

JUNK FOOD DETOX

Reset Your Body, Renew Your Mind

Sophie Domingues-Montanari, PhD

DISCLAIMER

The author made every effort to ensure the accuracy and reliability of the information provided in this book, but it is ultimately the responsibility of the reader to exercise discretion and judgment when applying the contents herein. It is highly recommended that readers seek guidance from qualified professionals, including healthcare practitioners or relevant specialists.

Furthermore, the author hereby absolves themselves of any liability for the outcomes that may stem from the use, application, or reliance upon the information provided within this book. This disclaimer encompasses, but is not limited to, any potential loss, injury, or damage – whether direct, indirect, incidental, consequential, or punitive – resulting from actions taken based on the information herein.

By accessing and utilizing the contents of this book, readers acknowledge and agree to indemnify and hold harmless the author from any and all claims, demands, or liabilities that may arise.

COPYRIGHT STATEMENT

Table of Contents

12

Introduction

Our body is not a garbage can. Yet, in our fast-paced, convenience-driven world, we often forget this vital truth. We stuff ourselves with junk food and harmful substances without considering the dire consequences. Our bodies are remarkable, capable of astounding feats when treated well, but they are not invincible. They deserve to be nourished and respected, not filled with unhealthy food. The impact of this lifestyle on our physical and mental health is profound. Processed foods, refined sugars, and artificial additives wreak havoc on our bodies, leading to chronic illnesses, weight gain, and plummeting energy levels. Mentally, these poor dietary choices can contribute to anxiety, depression, and brain fog. The damage is both immediate and long-term, eroding our overall quality of life and well-being. Acknowledging our neglect towards our own bodies is the first step towards change. It's easy to fall into patterns of convenience, choosing quick fixes over nutritious options. But recognizing that these choices are harmful empowers us to take responsibility for our health. This book urges you to confront these habits head-on and commit to treating your body with the care and respect it deserves.

Purposeful repetition is a key strategy in this book. We repeat core truths in different ways because they resonate with people differently. Hearing these messages multiple times solidifies healthier thinking and actions. By reminding ourselves of the importance of good nutrition and self-care, we can break free from harmful habits and adopt a more mindful approach to eating. This repetition ensures that one message will click with you, transforming your relationship with food. This book takes a tough love approach for genuine wake-up calls. If you bought this book, you already know something needs to change. The truth can be uncomfortable, but it's necessary for growth. This book doesn't sugarcoat the facts; it challenges you to face the reality of your choices and take steps toward better health. You have nothing to lose, and you're in good hands. This journey might seem daunting, but change is possible and rewarding. Even if you've failed before, this approach is different. With the right tools and guidance, you'll find it's not as hard as you think. By starting this detox, you're committing to yourself and your well-being. This book supports you every step of the way with the knowledge and advice you need to succeed.

This book offers an innovative approach to rewiring your brain and overcoming junk food addiction by understanding how you've been brainwashed, how junk food affects your brain chemistry, and breaking free from its grip. Just by reading this book until the end, you'll gain the insights and strategies needed to awaken your brain, making it easier to resist cravings and develop healthier eating habits. This journey is about changing the way you think about food and making choices that support long-term health. The goal is a holistic transformation of habits and lifestyle for lasting change. This is not a quick fix or temporary diet; it's a complete lifestyle overhaul addressing your nutritional needs, emotional relationship with food, and daily habits. By embracing this holistic approach, you can achieve sustainable health improvements, increased energy, a better mood, and a higher quality of life. This book will help you break the cycle of food addiction and make lasting changes that align with your wellness goals, leaving you feeling wonderful and finally free.

We're excited to embark on this journey with you and witness your transformation unfold. By taking steps to prioritize your health and well-being, you're investing in a future filled with vitality and joy. Remember, every positive change you make today contributes to a healthier tomorrow. Embrace this opportunity to reclaim control over your health and live your best life.

The Poisons in Your Pantry

In this section, we delve into the often-ignored dangers lurking in our pantry and fridge. We shine a spotlight on five major groups of foods and drinks that seriously affect our health: junk food, alcohol, sweets, processed meats, and sugary drinks. While the realm of harmful substances in our food is vast—from artificial additives to refined sugars—we focus on these categories because they're so prevalent in our diets and have significant health consequences. Our aim is to uncover these complexities and show how our daily food choices can either nourish us or hit us like a wake-up call or harm us.

The Truth About Junk Food

Junk food—those tempting snacks and meals promising instant satisfaction—may taste good in the moment, but they come with significant long-term consequences. Let's delve into the harsh reality without sugar-coating it.

Junk food is like a deceptive treat, loaded with sugars that promise a burst of energy but ultimately leave us feeling depleted. Imagine biting into a sugary donut or sipping a soda filled with high-fructose corn syrup. These foods are calorie-dense but nutrient-poor, creating a dangerous imbalance in our diet. The excess consumption of refined sugars overwhelms our system, causing rapid spikes in blood glucose levels. In response, the pancreas releases insulin in a desperate attempt to bring sugar levels back down.

However, this rollercoaster ride of sugar and insulin leads to repeated strain on our body's metabolic machinery. Over time, cells become resistant to insulin's effects, leading to insulin resistance—a precursor to type 2 diabetes. It's like trying to unlock a door with a rusty key; eventually, the lock stops responding altogether. The path to diabetes becomes clearer with every sugary snack consumed.

Moreover, junk food is often riddled with unhealthy fats, including trans fats lurking in fried foods and processed snacks. These fats not only contribute to weight gain but also wreak havoc on our cardiovascular system. Visualize these fats circulating in your bloodstream, adhering to artery walls like glue. LDL cholesterol—the "bad" cholesterol—levels soar, paving the way for atherosclerosis, a buildup of plaque that narrows arteries and restricts blood flow. The heart works harder, pumping against increased resistance, setting the stage for heart disease and strokes that can strike suddenly and silently.

Imagine your body after a sugary binge: a frantic surge of insulin coursing through veins, trying desperately to manage the onslaught of glucose. But the crash inevitably follows, leaving you drained and irritable, craving more of the quick-fix that got you here in the first place. This cycle of sugar highs and crashes not only drains physical energy but also destabilizes mood and cognitive function. Picture the emotional rollercoaster, swinging from euphoria to exhaustion within hours.

Beyond immediate effects, chronic exposure to refined sugars triggers a silent but deadly process: inflammation. Visualize inflammation as tiny fires raging within your body, sparked by excessive sugar consumption. These fires smolder silently, fanning the flames of metabolic syndrome—a constellation of conditions like high blood pressure, elevated blood sugar, and abnormal cholesterol levels. As inflammation spreads, it creates fertile ground for cancers to take root and thrive, a consequence of prolonged dietary neglect.

The toll of junk food extends beyond the physical realm, casting a shadow over mental well-being. Diets rich in processed foods have been linked to higher rates of mental health disorders such as depression and anxiety. Picture neurotransmitters—the brain's messengers—falling silent amidst the chaos of processed food overload. These foods starve the brain of vital nutrients and disrupt the delicate balance of gut microbiota, the army of microorganisms that safeguard gut health and influence brain function.

Imagine the gut-brain axis as a highway of communication, lined with traffic signals and neurotransmitter crossings. In a healthy gut, these signals flow smoothly, regulating mood and cognition with precision. But flood this highway with sugars and unhealthy fats, and traffic jams ensue. Disruptions in gut bacteria composition lead to increased inflammation, impairing neurotransmitter signaling and amplifying the risk of mood disorders. Visualize depression as a cloud that settles over your mind, fueled by the storm of inflammation raging within.

The Junkyard Stomach

Imagine your stomach as a pristine, well-maintained car engine. When you eat fresh fruits, vegetables, whole grains, and lean proteins, it's like fueling your engine with high-quality gasoline and maintaining it with clean oil. Your engine runs smoothly, efficiently, and lasts a long time.

Now, picture taking that same engine and pouring in a thick, greasy sludge mixed with chunks of rusted metal and broken glass. This sludge is equivalent to junk food: greasy fast food, sugary snacks, processed meats, and artificial additives. Imagine the sludge gumming up the gears, clogging the fuel lines, and corroding the metal components. The engine sputters, overheats, and eventually breaks down, unable to function properly.

Every time you consume junk food, it's like pouring that toxic sludge into your stomach. The sludge represents:

Greasy Fast Food: Imagine greasy, congealed fat sticking to the walls of your engine, clogging every crevice and slowing down every moving part.

Sugary Snacks: Visualize sugar granules acting like sandpaper, scratching and wearing down the

23

internal surfaces of the engine, causing it to grind and seize up.

Processed Meats and Additives: Think of rusted metal shards tearing through vital components, causing irreversible damage and accelerating the engine's decay.

This toxic sludge wreaks havoc on your stomach and body, leading to:

Obesity and Weight Gain: The sludge adds layers of unhealthy fat, just as grease builds up and slows down the engine.

Heart Disease and Diabetes: Imagine the sludge hardening the engine's pipes, mirroring how arteries become clogged with plaque, leading to heart attacks and strokes.

Mental Fog and Mood Swings: The engine misfires and stalls, just like your brain struggles with focus and mood stability due to poor nutrition.

By consuming junk food, you're essentially sabotaging your body's engine, leading to a breakdown of health and vitality. This vivid image of pouring sludge into a once-pristine engine serves as a powerful reminder of the destructive impact of unhealthy eating habits.

The Hidden Dangers of Sweets

Sweets, from tantalizing pastries to irresistible chocolates, occupy a cherished place in our hearts and cultural traditions. Yet beneath their alluring sweetness lies a stark reality about their impact on our health and well-being. Laden with refined sugars, unhealthy fats, and artificial additives, these treats set off a cascade of reactions within our bodies.

The rapid spikes in blood sugar levels caused by sweets pose a significant long-term threat. Regular consumption can lead to insulin resistance, where cells become less responsive to insulin—a crucial hormone for regulating blood sugar levels. This resistance not only heightens the risk of developing type 2 diabetes but also complicates its management for those already diagnosed. Additionally, excessive sugar intake contributes to weight gain by providing empty calories devoid of essential nutrients. This surplus often results in elevated cholesterol levels, placing added strain on cardiovascular health and increasing susceptibility to heart disease.

Beyond these physical health concerns, extensive research underscores the profound impact of sweets on mental well-being. Studies consistently establish a direct correlation between high sugar intake and mental health issues such as anxiety and depression. The initial surge of energy provided by sweets is typically followed by a crash, leaving individuals feeling drained, irritable, and emotionally unstable. This rollercoaster effect not only disrupts mood stability but also impairs cognitive function, diminishing our capacity to concentrate and make sound decisions.

So, why do we struggle to resist sweets despite understanding these risks? The answer lies in a complex interplay of cultural norms, social influences, and the brain's response to sugar. From childhood treats that evoke nostalgic memories to adult indulgences associated with celebrations and rewards, sweets are deeply woven into our social fabric and emotional experiences. Furthermore, the food industry capitalizes on our innate cravings for sugar, bombarding us with advertisements that portray sweets as irresistible and readily accessible temptations.

Understanding the Alcohol Trap

Let's strip away the illusions and have an honest conversation about alcohol. Often marketed as a gateway to relaxation and fun, it's time to confront the stark reality behind the allure of that buzz. Consider what alcohol truly inflicts upon our bodies—it wreaks havoc on our systems in profound and disturbing ways. Starting with our liver, our vital filter, alcohol swiftly clogs its pathways. From inducing fatty liver to progressing into cirrhosis, it paves the way for serious health complications. But its destructive path doesn't halt there. Alcohol spikes our blood pressure, disrupts our heart's steady rhythm, and dramatically heightens the risks of heart disease and stroke.

Now, let's zoom in on its impact on our brain, the very core of our being. Our brain, a marvel of biological engineering, keeps us sharp and in command. Yet, alcohol throws a wrench into this precision. Have you experienced how your thoughts become clouded after a few drinks? That's because alcohol slows down our brain's intricate communication pathways, interfering with the neurotransmitters that shuttle messages between brain cells. This slowdown not only dulls cognitive prowess but also

27

sabotages our judgment and decision-making abilities. Alcohol fundamentally rewires how our brain operates, undermining our capacity to swiftly and accurately process information. Tasks requiring focus and coordination grow increasingly daunting with each sip.

And sleep? Forget about a peaceful night's rest. While alcohol may initially lull you into sleepiness, it disrupts our sleep cycles by stifling REM sleep—the crucial phase for deep, rejuvenating rest that our bodies and minds crave. Despite logging more hours in bed, you wake up feeling drained and mentally foggy, unable to concentrate or perform at your best.

Let's confront the glaring issue: addiction. What may start as harmless relaxation can rapidly morph into dependency. Alcohol can seize control of your life, wreaking havoc on relationships, careers, and overall well-being.

We've been sold the myth that alcohol equals pleasure and leisure. However, this perception is a façade. While it may temporarily silence our inner voices, it exacts a heavy toll in the long run. It's time to dismantle the illusions surrounding alcohol. It doesn't enhance intelligence or happiness; instead, it clouds our minds, damages our bodies, and hinders us from living life to its fullest potential.

Unmasking Processed Meats: Understanding the Risks

Processed meats—those convenient, savory staples that often find their way onto our plates—are meticulously engineered for taste and longevity. Bursting with sodium, preservatives like nitrates, and unhealthy fats, they are designed to make meal preparation quick and easy. However, the cost to our health is anything but trivial. Regular consumption of these meats has been directly linked to a slew of serious health issues, including cardiovascular disease, hypertension from excessive salt intake, and a significantly heightened risk of certain cancers, particularly colorectal cancer.

Ever wondered why your favorite deli meats or sausages boast that unnaturally uniform color and flavor? It's not magic—it's chemistry at work. The nitrites and nitrates used in processing these meats can react under heat or during digestion to form harmful compounds known as nitrosamines. These compounds are well-documented carcinogens, and their presence in our diet is a ticking time bomb, escalating the risk of cancer with every bite.

But that's not the whole story. Let's delve deeper. Processed meats often contain a slew of artificial additives, including synthetic food colorings designed to give them that vibrant, appetizing look. These additives, like Red 40 or Yellow 5, might make the meat look more appealing, but they come with their own set of health risks. Studies have shown that these dyes can trigger allergic reactions and even exacerbate conditions like ADHD in children. The food industry's manipulation of color isn't just about aesthetics—it's about making these meats more enticing, masking their less savory components.

Moreover, the preservation methods used in processed meats can create a cocktail of harmful substances. Apart from nitrosamines, these meats are also laden with other carcinogenic compounds formed during processing and cooking, such as polycyclic aromatic hydrocarbons (PAHs) and heterocyclic amines (HCAs). These compounds are produced when meats are smoked, cured, or cooked at high temperatures, and they have been linked to an increased risk of cancer.

Imagine a sizzling sausage or a crispy bacon strip; with every bite, you're not just tasting the flavor but also a potential health hazard.

Processed meats are deeply ingrained in our diets and culinary traditions. They're convenient, versatile, and often cherished as comfort foods. However, just because something is familiar doesn't mean it's the best choice for our health. Let's challenge the status quo and rethink what we put on our plates. The next time you reach for that ready-made sandwich or those pre-cooked sausages, consider the hidden dangers lurking within. Our health deserves better. Let's choose whole, natural foods that nourish our bodies, not ones that slowly erode our well-being with every bite. It's time to reclaim our plates and make choices that truly support our health and vitality.

Sugary Beverages: The Bitter Truth

Sodas fizzing with promise, energy drinks fueling our days, and fruit juices seeming like healthy choices—these sugary beverages have firmly entrenched themselves in our lives with their enticing flavors and quick fixes. Yet, beneath their refreshing facades lie profound implications for our health and well-being.

These beverages deliver a powerful punch of sugar that can foster addictive consumption patterns and lead to serious health consequences. The excessive sugar intake from sodas, energy drinks, and fruit juices is intricately linked to rising rates of obesity, type 2 diabetes, cardiovascular diseases, and dental problems. They inundate our bodies with empty calories, devoid of essential nutrients, upsetting our metabolic equilibrium and paving the way for chronic illnesses. Beyond their sugar content, these drinks are loaded with artificial flavors, colors, and preservatives, additives that pose numerous health risks including metabolic disruptions and adverse reactions.

Energy drinks, in particular, are insidious in their allure. Marketed as performance enhancers, they promise to elevate energy levels, enhance focus, and prolong endurance. However, many of these drinks harbor elevated levels of caffeine and sugar, creating a potent cocktail of potential health hazards.

Caffeine, in moderation, can bolster alertness and alleviate fatigue. Yet, the quantities present in numerous energy drinks far surpass recommended daily limits, especially problematic for children and adolescents. Excessive caffeine consumption can provoke heightened heart rate, elevated blood pressure, and irregular heart rhythms. It can also exacerbate anxiety, trigger digestive issues, and disrupt sleep patterns, significantly impacting overall well-being.

The sugar content in energy drinks presents another major concern. Similar to sodas, these beverages are saturated with sugars that induce rapid spikes in blood glucose levels, fostering insulin resistance over time. This dual assault of high caffeine and sugar content often cultivates a dependency, compelling consumers to seek another drink to offset the inevitable crash following the initial surge of energy.

Furthermore, some energy drinks incorporate additional stimulants such as guarana and taurine, intensifying the effects of caffeine and placing further strain on the heart and nervous system.

While fruit juices are commonly perceived as healthier alternatives to sodas and energy drinks due to their natural origins and vitamin content, the truth is more nuanced, especially regarding their impact on blood sugar levels.

While fruit juices may offer essential vitamins and minerals, they lack the dietary fiber inherent in whole fruits. Fiber plays a pivotal role in slowing the absorption of sugars from fruits into the bloodstream. In whole fruits, fiber moderates the release of sugars, preventing rapid spikes in blood glucose levels.

Conversely, juicing fruits removes this crucial fiber content. As a result, the sugars in fruit juices are swiftly absorbed by the body, precipitating quick spikes in blood glucose levels akin to those triggered by sodas or high-sugar energy drinks.

For instance, a glass of orange juice may contain the natural sugars found in several oranges, but without fiber to temper digestion, these sugars are promptly absorbed into the bloodstream. This rapid elevation in blood sugar prompts the release of insulin to manage the influx of sugar. Over time, habitual consumption of fiber-devoid, high-sugar fruit juices can foster insulin resistance, weight gain, and heighten the risk of type 2 diabetes.

Additionally, the absence of fiber means that fruit juices do not impart the same sensation of fullness or satiety as whole fruits. This can lead to overconsumption of calories from juices, exacerbating the metabolic impact of high sugar intake.

Harmful Effects on the Body

Let's confront the harsh reality of the modern diet and its profound effects on us. It's not merely about gaining a few pounds or feeling a bit sluggish. The foods and beverages we consume daily wield a deep impact on both our bodies and minds. From physical afflictions such as obesity and heart disease to mental health challenges and disruptions in our microbiome, the repercussions extend far and wide. It's crucial to confront these realities directly and grasp the full extent of how our dietary decisions are eroding our health and overall well-being. It's time to acknowledge these truths and take proactive steps towards better health.

Obesity and Weight Gain

Obesity isn't just about carrying extra weight—it's a tangled health dilemma with deep-reaching consequences. It emerges when our bodies store excess fat, driven by a complex interplay of genetics, environment, and our daily choices, especially what we eat. Our modern diets, brimming with processed foods, sugars that spike like fireworks, and fats that clog arteries like sludge, fuel this epidemic. These foods dazzle with their flavors but leave us malnourished, packing on pounds while starving our bodies of the vital nutrients they crave.

Picture this: with every sip of a sugary drink or bite of a processed snack, we're overdosing on calories our bodies can't burn. It's like pouring gasoline onto a fire, our cells bursting at the seams with stored fat. These foods not only expand our waistlines but also corrode our health from within. Think of insulin, the key to regulating blood sugar, thrown out of balance by sugary onslaughts. Our bodies resist its signals, paving a dark path towards diabetes and metabolic chaos.

Obesity isn't just a number on a scale; it's a ticking time bomb for our health. Imagine the strain on our hearts as they pump harder against the cholesterol-clogged arteries. Picture the joints, groaning under the weight of excess pounds, as they struggle to bear the burden. And don't forget the silent invaders— cancers lurking in the shadows, fed by the surplus fat cells that breed inflammation and disease.

Living with obesity isn't just about feeling heavy; it's about living under a cloud of health risks. It steals our vitality, shortens our lives, and casts shadows over our future. This isn't about vanity—it's a stark reality that demands our attention, urging us to rethink what we eat and how we live.

Type 2 Diabetes

Imagine your body as a finely tuned machine, designed to process nutrients and maintain balance with precision. However, when you fill it with sugary beverages and processed foods, it's like pouring sand into a delicate mechanism. These foods disrupt your body's intricate dance with blood sugar, throwing insulin levels into disarray and setting the stage for a cascade of health issues.

Picture your bloodstream after a sugary drink or a processed meal—a surge of glucose floods your system, prompting a rapid release of insulin to bring levels back to normal. But with constant indulgence in these foods, your body's response mechanism starts to falter. Insulin resistance creeps in, where your cells become less responsive to insulin's signals, leaving glucose levels persistently elevated.

Now, envision your pancreas, tirelessly producing insulin to combat these spikes day after day. Over time, this relentless demand can exhaust its capacity, leading to a state where insulin production can no longer keep pace with the body's needs. This isn't just a theoretical concern—it's a pathway to chronic health conditions like type 2 diabetes, where blood sugar levels remain consistently high, wreaking havoc on your organs and overall well-being.

Living with insulin resistance and the specter of type 2 diabetes isn't just a matter of monitoring numbers—it's a battle against time and biology. It's about the silent struggle within your body, where every meal choice carries profound implications for your future health. This reality check isn't meant to scare but to underscore the urgency of making informed choices.

Cardiovascular Disease

Imagine your heart as the guardian of your vitality, tirelessly pumping life-giving blood through your body. Now, picture what happens when you regularly indulge in processed foods—a silent threat that chips away at your heart's resilience and sets the stage for serious health complications.

Consider the ingredients lurking within these convenient, often irresistible foods. They're packed with trans fats, saturated fats, and cholesterol—the notorious trio known for their role in cardiovascular sabotage. Visualize these substances as tiny saboteurs, infiltrating your arteries and triggering a dangerous process: plaque buildup. This accumulation narrows your arteries, constricting the flow of blood like a choked river, increasing your vulnerability to heart disease and stroke.

Now, shift your focus to sodium, the stealthy accomplice in processed foods. Designed to enhance flavor and prolong shelf life, sodium stealthily infiltrates your system with every bite. But excessive sodium isn't just about taste—it's a threat to your cardiovascular system. Picture your blood pressure rising under the strain of sodium overload, forcing your heart to work harder to pump blood efficiently. Over time, this relentless pressure can lead to hypertension—a silent predator that elevates your risk of heart attacks and strokes.

Visualize the cumulative effect of these dietary choices, each processed meal or snack contributing to a complex web of cardiovascular risks. Your heart deserves better—let's empower it with informed choices and a commitment to lasting well-being.

Digestive Issues

Your digestive system is a bustling ecosystem finely tuned to process and extract nutrients from the foods you consume. However, when bombarded with processed foods and sugary drinks, this vibrant ecosystem faces disruption akin to an unexpected storm.

Consider the importance of fiber in this ecosystem—the essential nutrient that acts as the backbone, facilitating smooth digestion and ensuring regularity. Without an ample supply of fiber from whole foods, there is potential for sluggish movement along the digestive tract, leading to discomfort and irregularity.

Now, think about the impact of artificial additives and preservatives as invasive species within this delicate ecosystem. These additives disturb the balance of beneficial bacteria, crucial for maintaining digestive health and bolstering the immune system. They disrupt the equilibrium of your gut microbiome, contributing to digestive issues such as bloating and indigestion.

Envision the cumulative effect on your digestive well-being: each processed meal and sugary beverage contributing to an ecosystem in turmoil, struggling to maintain its equilibrium. It's not just about short-term discomfort but nurturing a resilient digestive environment that supports your overall health and vitality.

Liver Damage

Your liver, a formidable guardian against toxins, faces an alarming challenge due to the prevalent consumption of processed foods and sugary beverages in today's diet. This vital organ acts as your body's primary filter, working ceaselessly to purify your bloodstream of harmful substances. However, the steady intake of processed foods and sugary drinks overwhelms its natural detoxification capabilities, straining its resilience and compromising its health.

Imagine your liver as a diligent janitor tasked with cleaning up a constantly messy room. Normally equipped to handle a moderate amount of debris, it thrives on a balanced diet rich in nutrients that support its functions. But when bombarded with processed foods lacking essential vitamins and minerals, and laden with synthetic additives, it struggles to keep up. The high levels of refined sugars, particularly from ubiquitous high-fructose corn syrup found in sodas and snacks, present a particularly daunting challenge.

High-fructose corn syrup floods your liver with fructose, a type of sugar that it struggles to process efficiently in large quantities. As a result, excess fructose undergoes a metabolic transformation, converting into fat that accumulates within liver cells. This buildup marks the onset of non-alcoholic fatty liver disease (NAFLD), a condition that begins silently, often without noticeable symptoms.

NAFLD can progress from simple fat accumulation to more severe stages of liver damage. Inflammation, known as steatohepatitis, sets in as liver cells become increasingly burdened and inflamed. If left unchecked, chronic inflammation can lead to the development of scar tissue, a hallmark of cirrhosis. Imagine your liver gradually becoming scarred and stiffened, impairing its ability to perform vital functions such as processing nutrients, filtering blood, and detoxifying the body.

Cirrhosis represents a critical stage of liver disease where irreversible damage occurs, posing significant risks such as liver failure and an increased susceptibility to liver cancer. Visualize your liver, once a resilient and adaptable organ, now struggling under the weight of chronic damage caused by dietary indiscretions.

Bone Health

You might not immediately connect your diet with your bones, but what you eat has a direct impact on your skeletal health. Your bones are the unsung heroes of your body's architecture, providing strength and stability to every move you make. Imagine them as the sturdy pillars of a grand building, resilient yet constantly in need of upkeep. What you eat plays a crucial role in this upkeep. Picture your diet as the builder's toolkit—filled with essential nutrients like calcium and vitamin D, crucial for maintaining bone health.

However, in today's fast-paced world, it's easy to rely on processed foods and sugary drinks that promise convenience but lack the nutrients your bones crave. These foods are like flashy, superficial decorations on a building—they might look appealing on the surface, but they don't provide the foundational support your bones need. They lack the vital ingredients that keep your bones strong and resilient.

Consider the impact of phosphates found in sodas—a hidden enemy that quietly saps calcium from your bones over time. Visualize them as stealthy underminers, weakening your bones' density and making them more prone to conditions like osteoporosis, where bones become brittle and susceptible to fractures.

As you journey through life, the importance of caring for your bones becomes increasingly clear. Without sufficient calcium and vitamin D, your bones struggle to maintain their strength, making fractures and other bone-related issues more likely. This concern isn't just for older adults; younger people who consume excessive sugary beverages may unknowingly compromise their bone health for the future.

In essence, your bones are more than just a framework—they're a dynamic, living part of your body that deserves attention and nourishment. Imagine your diet as the foundation for strong, resilient bones.

Dental Problems

We can't talk about sugary drinks without mentioning their impact on your teeth. Sugar, the main fuel for bacteria in your mouth, sparks a corrosive chain reaction. These bacteria eagerly convert sugar into acids that mercilessly attack your tooth enamel, the resilient armor shielding your teeth. Picture these acids as tiny, acidic raindrops continuously pelting your teeth, slowly but surely wearing down their defenses.

As you sip on sugary sodas, fruit juices, and energy drinks throughout the day, your teeth become immersed in a sugary bath. With each gulp, you're feeding the bacteria that thrive on sugar, intensifying their production of enamel-eroding acids. The result? Over time, your once-sturdy enamel weakens, paving the way for cavities to take root and gum disease to gain a foothold.

But it's not just sugar that spells trouble for your teeth. Artificial colors and acidic additives lurking in these beverages add to the onslaught. They not only stain your teeth, leaving behind stubborn discolorations, but also corrode enamel further. Imagine these additives as graffiti artists, leaving their mark and weakening the structural integrity of your teeth.

Despite your best efforts with toothbrush and floss, the relentless exposure to sugar and acids can overwhelm your dental defenses. It's like trying to defend a fortress besieged by constant attacks—while your defenses hold for a while, the persistent assault takes its toll over time.

To safeguard your dental fortress, consider the impact of every sip. Opt for water or alternatives without added sugars and acids to reduce the assault on your teeth. By making mindful choices, you strengthen your teeth's defenses, preserving their resilience against decay and sensitivity. Think of it as fortifying your smile against the daily onslaught, ensuring it remains vibrant and healthy for years to come.

Cheese: Nutritional Benefits and Considerations in Moderation

Cheese occupies a complex place in the realm of nutrition, straddling the line between being a rich source of nutrients and potentially contributing to unhealthy dietary habits when consumed in excess or in certain forms.

On one hand, cheese is prized for its nutritional benefits. It's a concentrated source of protein, calcium, phosphorus, and other essential nutrients important for bone health, muscle function, and overall vitality. Depending on the type of cheese, it can also provide significant amounts of vitamins such as vitamin A, vitamin B12, and riboflavin.

However, cheese is also high in saturated fats and sodium, which are two components often linked to adverse health outcomes when consumed in large quantities. Saturated fats, found predominantly in animal products like cheese, can contribute to elevated levels of LDL cholesterol ("bad" cholesterol) in the blood, potentially increasing the risk of heart disease if consumed excessively over time. The sodium content in cheese, particularly in processed varieties, can also contribute to high blood pressure when consumed in excess.

Moreover, the calorie density of cheese means that it can easily contribute to calorie intake surpassing energy needs, potentially leading to weight gain if not consumed in moderation. This aspect is particularly relevant in the context of modern diets that often include cheese in high-fat, high-calorie foods like pizzas, burgers, and processed snacks, where its nutritional benefits may be overshadowed by the overall caloric load and unhealthy additives.

In the broader context of junk food, cheese often features prominently due to its palatability and versatility in enhancing flavor and texture. It can be found in numerous processed foods that are high in saturated fats, sodium, and refined carbohydrates, such as cheeseburgers, nachos, and cheese-flavored snacks. These foods, while enjoyable in moderation, can contribute to a diet that lacks diversity in essential nutrients and exceeds recommended intake levels for less healthy components.

Therefore, while cheese can certainly be part of a balanced diet when consumed mindfully and in appropriate portions, its role in nutrition should be considered within the context of overall dietary patterns and health goals.

Joint Pain and Inflammation

Believe it or not, your diet can affect your joints too. Foods rich in sugar and unhealthy fats can ignite inflammation throughout your body, intensifying conditions like arthritis. This inflammation isn't isolated—it's a widespread problem that can permeate various areas of your body, exacerbating chronic conditions and causing persistent discomfort.

When you indulge in foods high in sugars and unhealthy fats, you're essentially fueling the fire of inflammation. Imagine inflammation as a smoldering blaze, sparked by sugary treats and fatty indulgences. These foods trigger immune responses that target not just your joints but also tissues throughout your body, amplifying pain and stiffness associated with arthritis.

Moreover, excess weight gained from consuming these empty calories further burdens your joints. Picture your joints as pillars supporting your body's weight. When laden with unnecessary pounds, these pillars strain under pressure, causing discomfort and reducing mobility.

Inflammation, however, is not merely a joint issue—it's a systemic concern affecting your overall well-being. By cutting back on processed foods and sugary drinks, you can help quell the flames of inflammation. This dietary shift supports your body's natural ability to combat inflammation, potentially alleviating symptoms and enhancing your quality of life.

Choosing whole, nutrient-rich foods over processed alternatives strengthens your body's defenses against inflammation. Imagine nourishing your body with foods that promote health and vitality, fostering an environment where inflammation subsides, and joint discomfort diminishes. This proactive approach not only benefits your joints but also enhances your overall health and vitality.

Compromised Immune System

Your immune system is a complex defense network that thrives on a diverse array of nutrients to function at its best. Unfortunately, processed foods and sugary drinks frequently fall short in providing these essential nutrients, leaving your body more susceptible to infections and illnesses.

Picture your immune system as a fortress fortified by vitamins, minerals, and antioxidants—essential nutrients that bolster its defenses against invading pathogens. Yet, when your diet is rich in processed foods and sugary beverages, this fortress becomes vulnerable. These foods often lack the vital nutrients needed to maintain a robust immune response, compromising your body's ability to fend off infections effectively.

High levels of sugar intake present a particular challenge. Imagine sugar as a saboteur within your fortress, weakening the guards (immune cells) and disrupting their ability to detect and destroy pathogens. This suppression of your immune response can make it harder for your body to combat infections, leaving you more susceptible to illnesses ranging from common colds and flu to more serious infections.

Moreover, chronic consumption of these unhealthy foods can lead to nutrient deficiencies over time. Picture your body as a garden deprived of essential nutrients— without proper nourishment, the soil becomes barren and unable to yield healthy crops (immune cells). As nutrient deficiencies mount, your immune defenses weaken, further diminishing your ability to ward off illnesses effectively.

This weakening of your immune system isn't just theoretical; it's a practical consequence of poor dietary choices. Imagine your body's immune system as a delicate balance. When this balance is disrupted by an inadequate diet, your defenses falter, leaving you more vulnerable to infections and illnesses that could otherwise be prevented.

Hormonal Imbalances

In addition to insulin disruption, diets rich in processed foods and sugars can profoundly affect other essential hormones in your body. Cortisol, often termed the stress hormone, serves as a conductor overseeing your body's response to stress. When you consume excessive sugars, cortisol levels can surge, creating a persistent state of stress within your body. This surge disrupts the delicate balance of hormones necessary for optimal health, akin to an overpowering crescendo disrupting an otherwise harmonious symphony.

Elevated cortisol levels not only trigger the body's stress response but also exert broader influences. They interfere with metabolism, promoting the storage of fat, particularly around the abdomen. Moreover, cortisol impacts mood and sleep patterns, contributing to feelings of anxiety, irritability, and disrupted sleep. This chronic stress state makes it challenging for the body to achieve equilibrium, affecting overall well-being.

Beyond cortisol, high sugar intake can disrupt the production and regulation of other critical hormones pivotal for overall health and vitality. For example, it can lead to imbalances in sex hormones such as estrogen and testosterone. In women, this disruption may contribute to conditions like polycystic ovary syndrome (PCOS). PCOS is characterized by irregular menstrual cycles, ovarian cysts, and hormonal imbalances that can impact fertility and increase the risk of long-term health issues like diabetes and cardiovascular disease.

Furthermore, diets high in processed foods and sugars can affect the thyroid gland, which produces hormones that regulate metabolism, energy levels, and body temperature. Excessive sugar consumption may disrupt thyroid hormone production and function, leading to conditions like hypothyroidism or hyperthyroidism, where the thyroid gland becomes underactive or overactive, respectively. These conditions can cause symptoms such as fatigue, weight changes, and mood disturbances, further complicating overall health.

Additionally, leptin and ghrelin, hormones that regulate hunger and appetite, can be affected by high sugar intake. Leptin signals to your brain that you're full, while ghrelin signals hunger. Diets high in sugars can disrupt this signaling mechanism, leading to increased hunger and potentially contributing to overeating and weight gain. The disruption of these critical hormones underscores the profound impact of diet on hormonal balance and overall health.

Cancer Risk

There's no doubt that what we eat and drink, including alcohol, can lead to cancer. For instance, processed meats have been conclusively linked to colorectal cancer. Studies show that additives like nitrates and nitrites in these meats can form nitrosamines during digestion, which are potent carcinogens. The International Agency for Research on Cancer (IARC) classifies processed meats as Group 1 carcinogens, placing them in the same category as tobacco and asbestos due to their strong link to cancer.

Sugary drinks are another serious culprit. These beverages contribute to obesity, which is a well-known risk factor for several types of cancer, including breast, ovarian, and prostate cancers. Excessive sugar intake leads to weight gain, insulin resistance, and elevated insulin levels, which can promote the growth of cancer cells. Furthermore, high blood sugar levels can cause chronic inflammation and oxidative stress, both of which are critical drivers in the development and progression of cancer.

Alcohol consumption is also a significant factor in cancer risk. Drinking alcohol increases the likelihood of developing cancers of the liver, mouth, throat, esophagus, and breast. Ethanol in alcohol is metabolized into acetaldehyde, a toxic compound that can damage DNA and proteins. The IARC classifies alcohol as a Group 1 carcinogen, affirming its direct role in cancer development. Alcohol also impairs the body's ability to absorb and utilize essential nutrients like folate, further increasing cancer risk.

Processed foods are laden with refined carbohydrates and unhealthy fats that contribute to chronic inflammation and oxidative stress, both of which play critical roles in cancer development. Chronic inflammation can damage healthy cells and tissues, providing a suitable environment for cancer cells to grow. Refined sugars and trans fats in these foods promote the production of inflammatory cytokines and reactive oxygen species, which can lead to DNA damage and cancerous mutations. Additionally, the lack of essential nutrients in these foods means your body misses out on vital antioxidants and phytochemicals found in whole foods, leaving you more vulnerable to the harmful effects of free radicals and other carcinogenic agents.

In addition to the above, there are other dietary elements that pose cancer risks. Fried foods, for example, contain acrylamide, a chemical formed when starchy foods are cooked at high temperatures, such as in frying or baking. Acrylamide is considered a probable human carcinogen by the IARC. Similarly, foods preserved by smoking or pickling, which often contain high levels of salt and chemicals, have been linked to stomach cancer.

High consumption of red meat, particularly when cooked at high temperatures (grilling or barbecuing), can lead to the formation of heterocyclic amines (HCAs) and polycyclic aromatic hydrocarbons (PAHs), both of which are carcinogenic. These compounds are created when muscle meat is cooked at high temperatures, and they have been linked to cancers of the colon, pancreas, and prostate.

Furthermore, diets low in fruits and vegetables are associated with a higher risk of developing cancer. These foods are rich in vitamins, minerals, and antioxidants that help protect cells from damage. Fiber, found in abundance in fruits and vegetables, also plays a role in reducing cancer risk, particularly colorectal cancer, by promoting healthy digestion and regular bowel movements.

By understanding the broad spectrum of dietary risks and the scientific mechanisms behind them, it becomes clear how vital it is to make healthier food and drink choices. Reducing intake of processed meats, sugary drinks, alcohol, fried foods, and red meat, while increasing consumption of nutrient-rich whole foods like fruits, vegetables, and whole grains, can significantly lower cancer risk. It's not just about adding years to your life, but also about improving the quality of those years by maintaining optimal health.

Is Describing Junk Food as Poison an Overstatement?

Describing junk food as "poison" can be seen as an exaggeration, but it does underscore the serious health risks associated with consuming these types of foods regularly and in large quantities. While poison typically refers to substances that can cause severe harm or death in small amounts, junk food doesn't have the same acute toxicity. However, it does share some similarities in terms of long-term detrimental effects on health.

Junk foods, such as highly processed snacks, sugary drinks, fast food, and foods high in unhealthy fats and additives, are typically low in essential nutrients and high in empty calories. Consuming them regularly can lead to a range of health issues, including obesity, type 2 diabetes, cardiovascular diseases, and various metabolic disorders. These foods often lack dietary fiber, vitamins, and minerals essential for overall health, leading to nutritional deficiencies over time.

Moreover, the ingredients commonly found in junk food, such as artificial trans fats, high fructose corn syrup, excessive sodium, and various food additives, have been linked to inflammation, oxidative stress, and damage to organs like the liver and heart. Excessive consumption of these ingredients can contribute to chronic conditions and increase the risk of developing serious illnesses later in life.

Furthermore, the addictive nature of junk food, driven by their high sugar, fat, and salt content, can lead to cravings and overconsumption. This cycle of addiction can contribute to weight gain, insulin resistance, and other metabolic disturbances, further exacerbating health problems.

While calling junk food "poison" may be provocative, it serves as a stark reminder of the potential harm these foods can cause when consumed in excess. The key takeaway is the importance of moderation and balance in diet, focusing on whole, nutrient-dense foods that support optimal health and well-being.

The Impact on Brain Health

Our brain, the control center for our thoughts, memories, emotions, and actions, is profoundly affected by what we consume. Harmful eating habits can impair cognitive function, erode memory, exacerbate depression and anxiety, and increase the risk of neurodegenerative diseases. Let's explore how poor dietary choices wreak havoc on our most vital organ. Understanding these impacts is crucial for making informed dietary choices that support a healthy, resilient brain.

Cognitive Function and Memory

Let's delve deeper into how what you eat and drink directly influences your brain's performance and, consequently, your quality of life. Imagine your brain as the command center of your entire being—a finely-tuned orchestra where every neuron plays a crucial role in orchestrating your thoughts, memories, emotions, and actions. When you nourish it with wholesome, nutrient-rich foods, it conducts this symphony with precision and clarity, allowing you to think quickly, remember vividly, and navigate life's challenges with ease.

However, introduce junk into this intricate orchestra—processed foods, sugary snacks, and alcohol—and it's akin to pouring discordant notes into the mix. The brain struggles to maintain harmony. Excessive sugar consumption, for example, leads to insulin resistance, disrupting the brain's ability to regulate glucose effectively. This metabolic upheaval doesn't just affect energy levels; it interferes with cognitive processes, leaving your brain foggy and sluggish, like trying to follow a melody through a thick fog.

Memory, one of the brain's most critical functions, suffers profoundly from poor dietary choices. Picture memories as delicate melodies—vivid experiences and cherished moments woven into the fabric of your life's soundtrack. When your brain lacks essential nutrients or is burdened by oxidative stress from processed foods, these melodies fade. The ability to recall details becomes fragmented, like trying to piece together a torn photograph. Studies emphasize that diets high in refined sugars diminish brain-derived neurotrophic factor (BDNF), a protein crucial for nurturing neurons and forging new memories. Without sufficient BDNF, your brain's capacity to retain information and form new connections diminishes, eroding the richness of your life's narrative.

Moreover, processed foods laden with trans fats and artificial additives disrupt the brain's intricate network of communication pathways. Imagine these pathways as intricate, finely-tuned instruments—when coated in inflammatory compounds, their signals falter and distort. The result is like listening to a symphony with intermittent static: thoughts that stutter, ideas that fail to connect, and memories that slip away before they can fully form.

In contrast, a diet rich in antioxidants—found abundantly in colorful fruits, vegetables, and whole grains—acts as a protective shield for your brain. These antioxidants sweep through your neural orchestra, neutralizing free radicals that threaten to distort its harmonious rhythm. Picture them as skilled musicians, skillfully conducting a symphony of clarity and vitality within your brain, preserving memories and enhancing cognitive resilience.

Alcohol, too, plays a dissonant role in this intricate composition. Chronic consumption shrinks the hippocampus, the brain's memory hub, and disrupts neurotransmitter balance. It's like listening to a melody played on a piano with missing keys—notes that should resonate clearly are muted or lost altogether. The result is a struggle to recall the past, organize thoughts coherently, and navigate everyday tasks with confidence.

Your brain is more than just an organ; it's the essence of who you are—the curator of your memories, the architect of your thoughts, and the orchestrator of your emotions. By choosing nourishment that supports its vitality—nutrient-rich foods, balanced meals, and mindful consumption—you empower your brain to perform at its peak, ensuring a symphony of clarity, sharp memory, and lasting well-being.

Depression and Anxiety

Depression and anxiety are not mere passing emotions but profound states that can envelop your entire being. Imagine waking up each day with a heavy cloak of sadness draped over your shoulders, making even the simplest tasks feel like climbing a mountain. Anxiety, on the other hand, is like a relentless storm brewing within, stirring up irrational fears and tightening your chest until each breath feels strained. These mood swings are like unpredictable weather patterns—sudden bursts of anger, waves of despair, and moments of numbness that can leave you feeling adrift in an emotional sea.

Your emotional well-being is not a luxury but a cornerstone of your existence, shaping how you perceive the world and interact with those around you. When you consume processed foods loaded with refined sugars and unhealthy fats, the impact on your mental well-being goes beyond physical health—it directly affects your emotional resilience and stability. These dietary choices initiate a chain reaction in your brain, akin to pouring fuel on a smoldering fire. The inflammation they trigger disrupts critical neurotransmitter functions, amplifying feelings of anxiety, depression, and mood swings, undermining your ability to maintain emotional balance amidst life's challenges.

Scientific research underscores the profound connection between diet and mental health. Diets high in refined sugars and unhealthy fats have been linked to increased inflammation in the brain, which disturbs the delicate balance of neurotransmitters like serotonin and dopamine. These neurotransmitters act as messengers within your brain, influencing mood regulation and emotional responses. Picture these messengers struggling to transmit clear signals amidst a storm of inflammation, intensifying feelings of anxiety and depression while diminishing your emotional resilience.

Furthermore, essential nutrients play a pivotal role in supporting mental well-being. Omega-3 fatty acids, abundant in fish, nuts, and seeds, are indispensable for maintaining optimal brain function and emotional stability. They bolster healthy brain cell membranes and enhance neurotransmitter function, fostering a stable mood and emotional equilibrium. A deficiency in these nutrients leaves the brain susceptible to heightened stress responses and mood instability. Visualize your brain cells striving to communicate effectively, their signals compromised by a lack of these vital nutrients. This deficiency not only heightens feelings of anxiety and depression but also hampers your ability to cope with everyday stressors, leaving you emotionally vulnerable and mentally overwhelmed.

While alcohol may seem to initially provide relief or relaxation, its enduring impact on mental health is profound and detrimental. Chronic alcohol consumption disrupts the intricate balance of neurotransmitters, impairing mood regulation and emotional stability. It's akin to navigating life with blurred vision, where clarity and emotional resilience become increasingly elusive.

Alcohol's influence on sleep exacerbates these issues. While it may induce initial drowsiness, it disrupts sleep quality by diminishing REM cycles and causing fragmented rest. Poor sleep patterns are closely linked to heightened risks of anxiety disorders, depression, and mood swings, leaving you emotionally fragile and mentally drained.

Beyond their physiological effects, poor diet and excessive alcohol consumption can precipitate psychological dependence and emotional distress. Using food or alcohol as coping mechanisms for stress or emotional pain engenders cycles of dependency that exacerbate mental health symptoms over time. Imagine being ensnared in a relentless cycle where each unhealthy choice momentarily soothes but ultimately deepens feelings of anxiety and depression.

Socially and emotionally, unhealthy eating habits and alcohol misuse strain relationships, undermine work performance, and erode overall quality of life. The resulting emotions of guilt, shame, and isolation perpetuate the cycle of anxiety and depression, fostering emotional instability and making everyday challenges seem insurmountable.

Neurodegenerative diseases

Neurodegenerative diseases, such as Alzheimer's and Parkinson's disease, represent a formidable challenge to the intricate workings of the brain. These conditions progressively erode the brain's structure and function, often leading to devastating consequences for cognition, mobility, and overall quality of life. Imagine your brain's neurons—once vibrant and interconnected— gradually succumbing to a relentless decay.

While nutrition plays a crucial role in managing these conditions, certain dietary choices can exacerbate their risk and progression. Research highlights specific dietary components that adversely affect brain health. Diets rich in saturated fats, commonly found in red meat, butter, and full-fat dairy products, as well as trans fats from processed and fried foods, significantly contribute to neuroinflammation and oxidative stress in the brain. These fats disrupt cellular processes, leading to the accumulation of beta-amyloid plaques and tau proteins. Beta-amyloid plaques interfere with neuron communication, while tau proteins disrupt internal transport systems, contributing to cell death—a process central to Alzheimer's disease and other neurodegenerative disorders, leading to cognitive decline and memory loss.

Moreover, consumption of refined sugars, prevalent in sugary beverages, candies, and high-glycemic index foods like white bread and pastries, causes rapid spikes in blood glucose levels and subsequent insulin release. Over time, sustained high blood sugar levels and insulin resistance trigger inflammatory responses in the brain, increasing oxidative stress and damaging neuronal structures. Elevated glucose levels also lead to the formation of advanced glycation end-products (AGEs) in the brain, exacerbating neuronal dysfunction and contributing to neurodegeneration.

Excessive alcohol consumption disrupts crucial neurotransmitter systems for synaptic transmission and cognitive function, such as glutamate and gamma-aminobutyric acid (GABA). Long-term alcohol abuse alters neuronal morphology, shrinking vital brain regions like the hippocampus and prefrontal cortex, essential for memory and executive function. Additionally, alcohol-induced oxidative stress and inflammation compromise the blood-brain barrier, facilitating the entry of harmful substances that further damage neurons. These combined effects accelerate cognitive decline and increase susceptibility to neurodegenerative diseases.

High salt intake is associated with hypertension, which raises the risk of vascular dementia by reducing blood flow to the brain. Hypertension can lead to small vessel disease and white matter lesions, impairing cognitive function over time. Processed foods containing additives, preservatives, and artificial sweeteners may contribute to neuroinflammation and oxidative stress, disrupting gut microbiota balance and potentially impacting brain health through the gut-brain axis.

Furthermore, excessive intake of iron, particularly from red meat, has been linked to oxidative stress and neurodegeneration. Iron accumulation in the brain promotes free radical production, contributing to neuronal damage and accelerating cognitive decline in susceptible individuals.

ADHD and Learning Difficulties

Research consistently highlights the detrimental effects of junk food on individuals with ADHD and learning difficulties. Consider this: diets rich in refined sugars from sugary drinks, candies, and processed foods send blood sugar levels on a rollercoaster ride of ups and downs. For those with ADHD, this isn't just a momentary sugar rush—it exacerbates hyperactivity, impulsivity, and challenges in maintaining focus. Moreover, prolonged consumption often intensifies mood swings, contributing to heightened anxiety and irritability, severely impacting daily functioning.

Beyond these immediate effects, junk food triggers inflammation throughout the body, including the brain. This chronic inflammatory state disrupts neural pathways crucial for attention and behavior regulation. Individuals with ADHD experience exacerbated difficulties in concentration and impulse control under such conditions.

Moreover, processed foods laden with additives such as sodium benzoate and artificial colors (like Red 40 and Yellow 5) can disturb neurotransmitter balance in the brain. These additives have been shown to interfere with dopamine levels, further complicating the ability to maintain focus and manage behavior effectively.

Additionally, caffeine from energy drinks and sodas disrupts sleep patterns, heightening restlessness and accelerating heart rate. The resulting sleep deprivation exacerbates symptoms of inattention and impulsivity during waking hours, compounding the challenges faced by individuals with ADHD.

Finally, excessive alcohol consumption disrupts critical neurotransmitter systems necessary for cognitive function, including dopamine and serotonin. Chronic alcohol abuse leads to neurotoxic effects that impair memory formation, information processing speed, and executive function. These impairments significantly worsen difficulties in concentration, task organization, and impulse management among individuals with ADHD and learning difficulties.

Self-Esteem and Confidence

Our self-esteem, the core of how we perceive and value ourselves, is deeply influenced by what we consume. Imagine self-esteem as a resilient structure built on a foundation of healthy habits and self-care. When we nourish our bodies with wholesome, nutrient-rich foods, this foundation becomes strong and supportive. However, when we introduce junk food—processed snacks, sugary drinks, and alcohol—into our lives, it's like pouring acid onto this foundation. The structural integrity weakens, leading to a cascade of negative effects on our mental and emotional well-being.

Eating poorly erodes our confidence and self-respect. When we consistently choose unhealthy foods, we may experience weight gain, skin issues, and low energy levels, all of which can contribute to a negative self-image. Imagine looking in the mirror and seeing the effects of poor nutrition staring back at you. The frustration and disappointment can be overwhelming, chipping away at your self-esteem day by day. And then there's the guilt. After indulging in junk food, the immediate gratification is often followed by a wave of remorse and self-reproach. You know these choices are harming your body and mind, yet the cycle of poor eating continues, deepening the guilt and further eroding your self-worth.

Moreover, the link between diet and mood is undeniable. Diets high in refined sugars and unhealthy fats can lead to mood swings, irritability, and feelings of anxiety and depression. These emotional states are detrimental to self-esteem, making it difficult to maintain a positive outlook on oneself and life. Picture your mood as a delicate balance—when disrupted by poor nutrition, it becomes a rollercoaster of highs and lows, leaving you feeling unsteady and unsure of yourself.

Processed foods laden with trans fats and artificial additives further complicate matters. These substances disrupt the brain's chemistry, interfering with neurotransmitter production and signaling. The result? A mind clouded by negative thoughts and self-criticism, struggling to find clarity and positivity. It's like trying to navigate through a thick fog, with every step mired in self-doubt and insecurity.

On the other hand, recognizing the destructive impact of poor dietary choices on self-esteem is the first step toward reclaiming your confidence. By choosing foods that support your mental and emotional health, you can rebuild the foundation of your self-esteem. Picture nourishing your body with vibrant, nutrient-dense foods that fortify your mind and spirit, enabling you to stand tall and face the world with confidence. Every positive choice weakens the hold of guilt, replacing it with pride and a renewed sense of self-worth.

The Devastating Impact of Junk Food

When you're struck down by a minor illness like a strep throat or a cold, it's as if a heavy fog settles over your entire being. Your throat feels like it's on fire, every swallow an agonizing journey through sandpaper. Your head throbs with each heartbeat, your sinuses are a congested mess, and your body aches as if you've been trampled by a stampede. Even the simplest tasks become monumental challenges, as if you're wading through molasses in slow motion. The fatigue wraps around you like a suffocating blanket, draining every ounce of energy and leaving you feeling utterly defeated.

Now, amplify that discomfort, that sense of being trapped in a body that's turned against you, to a magnitude that feels insurmountable. Imagine facing something far more sinister, like cancer. It's not just physical agony; it's a relentless assault on every aspect of your existence. Cancer grips you with a vice-like intensity, its claws sinking deep into your flesh and soul. The pain becomes a constant companion, gnawing away at your strength and resolve. Nausea overwhelms you, a bitter taste lingering in your mouth, while waves of fatigue crash over you like a relentless storm.

With cancer, it's not just the body that suffers. It's the mind and spirit that bear the brunt of the battle. Fear and uncertainty loom large, casting long shadows over your hopes and dreams. Every day becomes a tightrope walk between hope and despair, courage and vulnerability. The treatments meant to save you—chemotherapy, radiation, surgery—exact a toll that goes beyond physical discomfort. They strip away your hair, your vitality, your sense of normalcy, leaving behind a hollow shell of what once was.

In contrast, junk food may seem harmless—a momentary pleasure, a quick fix for cravings. But its insidious effects are no less devastating. Picture the allure of a greasy burger dripping with saturated fats, a mountain of fries doused in salt, or a sugary drink that promises a fleeting rush of sweetness. Yet, these foods are laden with hidden poisons— trans fats that clog your arteries, sugars that hijack your metabolism, additives that disrupt your body's delicate balance.

Consuming junk food isn't just about indulgence; it's about surrendering to a cycle of addiction and harm. Each bite chips away at your health, paving the way for obesity, diabetes, heart disease, and a host of other chronic illnesses. The consequences ripple outward, affecting not just your physical well-being but your emotional resilience and mental clarity. It's a betrayal of your body's innate wisdom, a compromise of your vitality and longevity.

In the face of these stark realities, the choice becomes clear. Opt for nourishment that fortifies your body and honors your well-being. Choose foods that energize, heal, and sustain—a vibrant spectrum of fruits, vegetables, whole grains, and lean proteins. Embrace hydration as a cornerstone of your health, a lifeline that supports every cellular function. Reject the toxic allure of junk food, reclaiming your power to thrive, not just survive. As we navigate the complexities of health and nutrition, let's remember that every choice matters.

Exploring the Microbiome

Now let's talk about something that doesn't get nearly enough attention: the gut microbiome. This microscopic community living in our digestive tract is like a bustling city of bacteria, viruses, and fungi that keeps us healthy. It's not just about digestion; it's about overall health. But our modern diets are wreaking havoc on this delicate ecosystem, leading to a cascade of health issues.

The Hidden Powerhouse

Our gut is home to trillions of microorganisms that play a crucial role in our health. These microorganisms are like tiny workers, breaking down food, producing vitamins, and protecting us from pathogens. A healthy gut microbiome is a balanced one, where beneficial bacteria thrive and keep the harmful ones in check. When this balance is disrupted, it leads to dysbiosis, setting off a chain reaction of health problems.

Processed foods are like a wrecking ball to the gut microbiome. Loaded with sugar, unhealthy fats, and artificial additives, these foods promote the growth of harmful bacteria while wiping out the good ones. High sugar intake feeds harmful bacteria like Clostridium and Escherichia coli, allowing them to dominate. This imbalance, or dysbiosis, wreaks havoc on our digestive system.

Ever felt bloated, gassy, or just plain uncomfortable after eating junk food? That's your gut microbiome crying for help. Dysbiosis leads to poor digestion, nutrient malabsorption, and a host of digestive issues. Harmful bacteria produce gas and other byproducts that irritate the gut lining, causing inflammation and discomfort.

The damage doesn't stop at digestive discomfort. Chronic inflammation from dysbiosis is a breeding ground for serious diseases like inflammatory bowel disease (IBD), irritable bowel syndrome (IBS), and even colorectal cancer. The toxins produced by harmful bacteria can induce mutations in gut lining cells, leading to cancer. It's a silent killer lurking in our guts, waiting to strike.

Immune System Under Siege

The immune system is the body's defense network against harmful invaders such as bacteria, viruses, fungi, and parasites. Think of it as a complex and highly organized army that patrols every part of your body, constantly on alert to detect and eliminate threats. Its importance cannot be overstated because without a properly functioning immune system, our bodies would be defenseless against infections and diseases.

Your gut microbiome isn't solely about digestion; it serves as your first line of defense against illness. It functions as the nerve center of your immune system—an essential command post where a vibrant microbiome educates and fine-tunes your body's defenses, adeptly distinguishing friend from foe.

However, dysbiosis disrupts this symphonic balance. It's akin to throwing a wrench into the gears, derailing the meticulously coordinated immune response. Junk food serves as the saboteur, packed with sugars, unhealthy fats, and artificial additives that upset this delicate equilibrium.

When dysbiosis takes root, it doesn't merely weaken your immune system; it cripples it. Your body struggles to discern between allies and threats, leaving you more susceptible to infections and illnesses. This vulnerability isn't theoretical; it's stark reality. Envision your once-vigilant immune cells now sluggish and bewildered, overwhelmed by invading harmful bacteria.

But that's not the end of it. Dysbiosis can incite an immune system in overdrive—an unyielding onslaught of inflammation that knows no bounds. This chronic inflammation isn't just discomforting; it's a ticking time bomb for autoimmune diseases. Picture your body's defenses turning against itself, attacking healthy tissues and organs, fueling conditions like inflammatory bowel disease and rheumatoid arthritis.

In this battleground of the gut, every mouthful of junk food plays a pivotal role. It nourishes the wrong bacteria, starves the beneficial ones, and triggers a domino effect of health catastrophes. It's not just about feeling bloated or sluggish after a meal; it's about the silent havoc unfolding within—cell mutations, persistent inflammation, and an immune system compromised and adrift.

The Gut-Brain Connection: A Two-Way Street

Ever heard the saying, "Trust your gut"? It's more than just a saying; it delves into the profound connection between our gut and brain via the gut-brain axis—a critical pathway where trillions of microorganisms in our gut dynamically interact with our brain functions. These microorganisms are not passive bystanders; they actively synthesize neurotransmitters like serotonin and metabolites that intricately influence our mood, cognition, and overall mental well-being.

However, when you consistently subject this complex ecosystem to junk food—loaded with excessive sugars, unhealthy fats, and synthetic additives—it's akin to dumping toxic waste into a pristine river. These dietary choices disrupt the delicate balance of your gut microbiota, nurturing harmful bacteria while suppressing the essential, beneficial microbes crucial for optimal neurological function.

Dysbiosis, the resultant imbalance from such dietary indulgences, transcends mere digestive discomfort. It profoundly disturbs the gut-brain axis, impairing the production of neurotransmitters essential for regulating mood and stress responses, such as serotonin and GABA. Instead of feeling emotionally stable, you may find yourself battling mood swings, heightened anxiety, or even symptoms of depression.

Moreover, dysbiosis initiates a cascade of chronic inflammation—a corrosive force that originates in your gut and permeates into your brain. This inflammatory response disrupts delicate neural processes, compromising cognitive function and potentially escalating the risk of debilitating neurodegenerative diseases like Alzheimer's and Parkinson's.

To compound these issues, dysbiosis compromises the integrity of the intestinal barrier, often referred to as "leaky gut." This compromised barrier allows toxins, harmful bacteria, and undigested food particles to leak into your bloodstream, triggering systemic inflammation that further undermines brain health. It's a vicious cycle where poor dietary choices not only devastate gut health but also perpetuate a decline in neurological function.

Scientifically, research underscores the detrimental impact of high-sugar diets on the gut microbiota, promoting the growth of pathogenic bacteria like Clostridium difficile and Escherichia coli. These microbes thrive on sugars, exacerbating dysbiosis and contributing to systemic inflammation. Furthermore, the excessive consumption of unhealthy fats alters gut microbial diversity and function, hindering the production of beneficial metabolites crucial for brain health.

Similarly, the intake of alcohol disrupts the gut microbiota, promoting dysbiosis and compromising intestinal barrier function. Alcohol metabolites can induce inflammation in the gut lining, contributing to systemic inflammation and neuroinflammation. Chronic alcohol consumption also impairs the synthesis and function of neurotransmitters like dopamine and serotonin, further exacerbating mood disorders and cognitive impairment.

The Dilemma of Popular Yet Harmful Substances

So far, we've examined in detail the harmful effects of certain foods, alcohol, sugary drinks, and other dietary choices on our bodies and minds. Whether this information was already familiar or just confirmed your gut feelings, you now clearly understand the risks—from obesity and diabetes to mood disorders and gut dysbiosis. But amidst this understanding, a nagging question remains: why are these unhealthy options still so pervasive? It's a puzzling reality that confronts us daily. Despite knowing the damage they can cause, why do these products—loaded with sugars, unhealthy fats, and artificial additives—continue to dominate our diets and grocery store aisles? It's not just their presence; it often seems they're becoming more ubiquitous. Could it be convenience, our taste preferences, or something deeper embedded in our culture and economic systems? Let's uncover the underlying reasons behind their persistent popularity. By unraveling these complexities, we aim to illuminate why these less-than-ideal choices thrive in our modern lifestyles despite their well-documented health risks.

Governmental Inaction: The Regulatory Landscape

One major reason behind the pervasive presence of these foods and drinks? Governmental inaction. Yes, you heard that right. The regulations and policies intended to govern what's sold in stores and marketed to us often fail to adequately protect our health.

Take sugary drinks, for example. Despite overwhelming evidence linking them to obesity and diabetes, there's little regulation on the amount of sugar that can be crammed into a can of soda or a bottle of juice. Manufacturers can freely pump these beverages full of sugar without facing strict limits, flooding the market with these high-sugar options.

Moreover, when health experts raise concerns about processed meats or the risks of excessive alcohol consumption, the process of implementing changes or setting clear guidelines can drag on for years within regulatory bodies. This sluggishness in taking action leaves consumers in a landscape where unhealthy choices are frequently more convenient and cheaper than healthier alternatives.

This prolonged regulatory process is driven by various factors: rigorous scientific research is needed to establish the health impacts of specific foods and ingredients; extensive public consultations are required to balance diverse stakeholder perspectives; industry lobbying efforts can delay or dilute proposed regulations; administrative challenges like budget constraints and legal complexities further hinder swift action; and political considerations often influence policy decisions, impacting the prioritization of public health over economic interests.

Consequently, our store shelves and advertising spaces remain packed with products that contribute to serious health issues, while efforts to promote and regulate healthier options often fall behind. The implications are staggering: we're stuck with a food environment that undermines public health despite widespread knowledge of the risks associated with these dietary choices.

In essence, the availability and promotion of these harmful foods aren't due to their benefits to our well-being—they persist because governmental regulations often fail to prioritize public health over industry interests. It's a stark reality that demands scrutiny and advocacy for change toward healthier, more responsible food policies.

Industry Influence: Marketing Might

Big food and beverage companies invest billions annually in sophisticated marketing campaigns aimed at convincing us that their products are not just enjoyable but essential for our diets and lifestyles. Consider the colorful advertisements for sugary cereals strategically placed during children's favorite TV shows, or the endorsements by celebrities promoting energy drinks as vital for peak performance and vitality. These tactics forge strong emotional connections between these products and positive experiences, making them difficult to resist—despite well-documented health risks like excessive sugar consumption and energy drink additives.

However, industry influence extends beyond advertising. Through powerful lobbying efforts, these companies shape food labeling regulations, advocate for lenient advertising guidelines, and influence school nutrition programs, prioritizing profit margins over public health. This contributes to a landscape where unhealthy foods and drinks dominate store shelves and permeate our daily lives.

We are subtly manipulated by these tactics, effectively brainwashed into believing that these products are not only acceptable but desirable choices. The relentless bombardment of persuasive advertising, coupled with industry-friendly policies, creates a pervasive cultural norm where junk food and sugary drinks are normalized as convenient, affordable, and socially acceptable options.

This pervasive marketing and lobbying power underscores the profound challenges in promoting healthier alternatives and enacting stricter regulations to safeguard public health. It's a complex interplay where consumer choice, industry influence, and regulatory policies converge, shaping the food environment we navigate every day. Navigating this landscape requires a critical examination of the forces at play and a concerted effort to advocate for policies that prioritize public health over corporate interests, demanding greater transparency, stricter regulations, and informed consumer empowerment.

Coffee: Unveiling its Health Impacts and Hidden Pitfalls

Coffee occupies a unique position in the realm of nutrition and dietary habits, often straddling the line between being a beloved beverage and occasionally being associated with unhealthy consumption habits when additives and excess sugar are included. On its own, coffee is a naturally low-calorie beverage that contains several bioactive compounds, including caffeine, chlorogenic acids, and antioxidants. Caffeine, the most well-known component of coffee, acts as a central nervous system stimulant that can enhance alertness, concentration, and mood when consumed in moderation. Some studies also suggest potential health benefits of coffee, such as reducing the risk of certain diseases like Parkinson's disease, Alzheimer's disease, type 2 diabetes, and liver cirrhosis. However, coffee's classification as a junk food or unhealthy beverage often stems from the additives and ingredients that people commonly pair with it.

Sugar: Adding excessive amounts of sugar to coffee can significantly increase its calorie content and contribute to weight gain and metabolic issues. Sweetened coffee beverages, such as flavored lattes, mochas, and frappuccinos, can contain high levels of added sugars, which may outweigh the potential health benefits of coffee itself.

Creamers and Flavored Syrups: Creamers and flavored syrups used to enhance the taste of coffee can be high in saturated fats, sugars, and artificial additives. These ingredients can undermine the nutritional value of coffee and contribute to an unhealthy diet if consumed regularly in large quantities.

Processed Coffee Drinks: Many commercially available coffee drinks, such as energy drinks or pre-mixed coffee beverages, often contain added sugars, artificial flavors, and preservatives. These products may provide a quick energy boost but can also contribute to excess calorie intake and may not offer the same health benefits as plain, black coffee.

In moderation and without excessive additives, coffee can be a part of a healthy diet for many individuals. It's a source of hydration, antioxidants, and potentially beneficial bioactive compounds. However, excessive consumption of coffee loaded with sugars and unhealthy additives, can contribute to negative health outcomes such as weight gain, dental issues, and metabolic disturbances.

Cultural Norms and Convenience

Let's get real: cultural norms, family traditions, and the sheer convenience of processed foods and sugary drinks heavily influence what we eat. In our fast-paced world, convenience often trumps health considerations. Whether it's grabbing a soda from a vending machine or ordering a pizza after a hard day of work, these choices are deeply ingrained in our social lives and daily routines.

Tradition plays a role too. For generations, certain foods have been staples in our diets, passed down through families and celebrated in cultural events. These traditions create strong emotional ties to foods that may not always be the healthiest choices.

Our education also plays a part. From childhood, we're often taught that these foods are normal and acceptable. Schools may serve processed meals due to convenience and budget constraints, reinforcing the idea that these choices are acceptable.

But here's the kicker: just because something has been done a certain way for a long time doesn't make it right. Processed foods and sugary drinks offer zero nutritional value and do not benefit our well-being in any circumstance. They're loaded with sugars, unhealthy fats, and additives that contribute to obesity, diabetes, and a host of other health problems.

Their popularity isn't due to their nutritional value—it's driven by convenience, aggressive marketing, and our desire for quick fixes. These foods are easy to find, cheap to buy, and heavily promoted, making them hard to resist even when we know they're not good for us.

To break free from this cycle, we need to challenge these norms and traditions. We must advocate for environments that support healthier choices and empower individuals to prioritize their health over convenience and outdated cultural practices. It's time to rethink how we eat, educate ourselves and our families about healthier options, and reclaim our well-being from the grip of convenience and tradition.

Economic Factors: Affordability and Accessibility

Last but not least, economic factors play a significant role in the prevalence of these harmful foods and drinks. These products aren't just omnipresent—they're aggressively priced to outcompete nutritious options like fresh fruits, vegetables, and lean proteins.

Consider the harsh reality of food deserts, where nutritious choices are scarce or non-existent. Every day, millions of individuals confront a stark choice: opt for cheap, calorie-dense meals or invest more money and time into healthier options. Economic constraints often force families to prioritize immediate financial concerns over long-term health, perpetuating a cycle of poor dietary habits.

Adding insult to injury, government subsidies artificially deflate the costs of ingredients like corn syrup and cheap grains, which are then heavily utilized in processed foods and sugary drinks. These subsidies make unhealthy choices irresistibly affordable, particularly for those on tight budgets. It's a system that actively promotes the consumption of foods devoid of nutritional value, fueling the epidemic of obesity, diabetes, and other chronic illnesses.

Moreover, the economic machinery behind food production prioritizes efficiency and profit margins over public health. This results in a glut of processed foods inundated with sugars, fats, and additives that contribute to poor health outcomes. From fast food chains to supermarket shelves, the ubiquity of these products serves as a daily reminder of economic priorities that disregard the well-being of consumers.

These economic forces perpetuate a food environment where junk food isn't just an option—it's often the default choice. They shape dietary preferences, dictate access to nutritious foods, and reinforce unhealthy habits ingrained in societal norms. Breaking free from this cycle requires confronting the economic structures that perpetuate it, advocating for equitable food access, and demanding policies that prioritize health over profit.

In essence, the prevalence of junk food isn't merely a matter of personal choice—it's a consequence of economic policies that prioritize corporate interests over public health.

Common Objections

"If junk foods are bad for me, why do they taste so good?"

Ah, the paradox of taste versus health. It's a compelling question with a complex answer rooted in biology and food industry practices.

Firstly, our taste preferences are evolutionarily wired to favor foods that are calorie-dense and high in sugar and fats. This preference likely stems from our ancestors' need to seek out energy-dense foods to survive in environments where food scarcity was common. Our taste buds haven't evolved to distinguish between natural sugars found in fruits and vegetables and the refined sugars added to processed foods, which can hijack our taste receptors and create a craving for sweetness.

Secondly, the food industry has mastered the art of enhancing flavors to make foods irresistibly tasty. Processed foods are often engineered with precise combinations of sugars, fats, salts, and artificial additives to optimize their palatability. This creates a sensory experience that triggers pleasure centers in our brains, similar to how addictive substances can hijack our brain's reward system.

Moreover, marketing plays a significant role in shaping our perceptions of taste and desirability. Colorful packaging, catchy slogans, and celebrity endorsements create powerful associations between certain foods and positive emotions or experiences. These tactics influence our purchasing decisions and reinforce the idea that indulging in these foods is not just enjoyable but also socially acceptable.

However, despite their appealing taste, these foods often lack essential nutrients and can contribute to a range of health problems when consumed in excess. They can lead to weight gain, metabolic disorders like diabetes, cardiovascular diseases, and even affect mental health by causing fluctuations in mood and energy levels.

So, while junk foods may taste good due to a combination of biological factors and industry tactics, it's crucial to remember that their taste doesn't equate to nutritional value or benefit to our well-being. Making informed choices about what we eat involves understanding the long-term consequences of our dietary habits and prioritizing foods that nourish our bodies rather than just satisfying our taste buds in the moment.

"Life is boring without pizza and beer."

It's understandable to feel that way initially! Pizza and beer are often seen as a way to unwind, socialize, and enjoy life with friends— it might even be your go-to choice for hanging out. But it's worth considering whether you truly enjoy the taste of pizza and beer, or if you've simply grown accustomed to associating them with relaxation and good times. Our sense of enjoyment can evolve as we explore new experiences and options.

Sometimes, personal growth means distancing yourself from certain influences. Picture this scenario: You've decided to quit smoking and commit to a healthier lifestyle. Imagine being surrounded by friends who not only support your decision but also share your values and dreams. They're the ones suggesting outdoor adventures, spontaneous outings, and lively conversations over fresh smoothies. Together, you discover new hobbies, uncover hidden trails, and celebrate every milestone with encouragement.

Now, contrast that with the alternative: lingering around smokers, their clothes permeated with the scent of tobacco, their breaks filled with cigarettes and mediocre coffee. The sight and smell no longer align with your newfound clarity and vitality. It's not just about avoiding secondhand smoke; it's about surrounding yourself with positivity and people who inspire and uplift you on your journey towards a healthier lifestyle.

Similarly, being in environments where alcohol flows freely—bars, parties, social gatherings—bombards you with sensory cues that amplify alcohol's pervasive presence. The air thickens with the stale stench of beer and potent spirits, clinging to everything and lingering long after the party ends.

In these scenes, you see people clutching glasses and bottles, their movements growing unsteady as the night wears on. Conversations fluctuate between uproarious laughter and slurred speech, punctuated by the clinking of glasses and the constant flow of drinks. The atmosphere pulses with an energy centered around alcohol—an allure fueled by promises of relaxation, social bonding, and a brief escape from reality.

Yet beneath this facade of camaraderie and euphoria lies an undercurrent of vulnerability and danger. The carefree demeanor often masks the potential for reckless behavior, impaired judgment, and the looming threat of addiction. For many, these settings become breeding grounds for habits that undermine physical health, strain relationships, and erode personal well-being over time.

Navigating these environments requires a nuanced balance between social acceptance and personal responsibility—a choice that weighs immediate pleasures against long-term consequences. Choosing friends who share your values and prioritize healthy choices isn't just about breaking old habits; it's about embracing a vibrant, fulfilling life where each moment is enriched with positivity and endless possibilities.

Ultimately, finding this balance and exploring new experiences, forming meaningful connections, can broaden your enjoyment of life beyond pizza and beer, guiding you toward becoming the best version of yourself.

Unveiling Alcohol's Toxic Legacy

Many perceive alcohol as a crutch—a social lubricant that eases nerves and fosters camaraderie. It promises temporary relief from stress, anxiety, and inhibitions. However, beneath this facade lies a harsh reality: alcohol is not a friend but an adversary.

At first glance, it seems to offer solace—a temporary escape from life's pressures. It dulls the edges of discomfort and social awkwardness, providing a fleeting sense of relaxation and confidence. Yet, this perceived relief is illusory. Alcohol's effects are short-lived and followed by consequences that often outweigh its temporary benefits.

Psychologically, alcohol can create a cycle of dependence. It offers an artificial sense of relief that can quickly turn into a crutch—an emotional prop relied upon to cope with stress, loneliness, or insecurity. Over time, this reliance deepens, masking underlying issues rather than addressing them.

Physiologically, alcohol exacts a toll on the body with each use. It disrupts neurotransmitter balance, impairs cognitive function, and undermines physical health. Regular consumption can lead to addiction, liver disease, cardiovascular issues, and a host of other health problems.

Socially, alcohol's role as a crutch can strain relationships and erode self-esteem. What begins as a social lubricant can morph into excessive drinking, leading to embarrassing behavior, conflicts, and isolation from loved ones.

Ultimately, recognizing alcohol's true nature is crucial. It is not a reliable ally but a deceptive adversary—a substance that promises relief but delivers harm. By acknowledging this reality and seeking healthier coping mechanisms, individuals can break free from the cycle of dependency and reclaim control over their well-being.

"Is life even worth living if I can't eat what I want?"

Let's unpack that. When we indulge in junk food, don't we often find ourselves feeling a bit off afterward? Maybe it's a stomach ache or feeling dizzy from sugary drinks. Perhaps it's regret over things said while drunk that we wouldn't normally say. Do we truly enjoy eating food that leaves us feeling physically sick and emotionally ashamed?

Consider the speed at which we consume these foods. A burger disappears in a minute, yet eating a vegetable feels like it takes ages. Why is that? Junk food isn't designed to nourish and satisfy us. Instead, it often leaves us hungry again an hour later, trapped in a cycle of cravings and dissatisfaction.

Think about those perfectly uniform fries or chicken nuggets that contain who knows what parts of the animal. Are we really enjoying food that's been processed with bleach to look identical, devoid of its natural qualities? And what about chocolate spread that's 90% sugar—does that truly satisfy our taste buds or just spike our sugar levels?

Now, let's talk about those nights out where alcohol flows freely. Does it feel like you're truly enjoying yourself when you wake up feeling sick and regretful? Consider the aftermath of excessive drinking—nausea, headaches, and the shame of not remembering what you said or did.

So, let's ask the question: Do you really enjoy eating junk? Is it worth sacrificing your well-being and happiness for a fleeting moment of taste? Life is about more than the immediate gratification of junk food and excessive indulgence. It's about feeling vibrant, energized, and clear-headed—qualities that come from making choices that truly nourish your body and soul.

Choosing to prioritize your health isn't about deprivation; it's about self-respect and setting yourself up for a life filled with vitality and joy. That's what makes life worth living— embracing choices that honor your well-being and allow you to thrive in every aspect of life.

"But food and alcohol help me relax after a long day."

Food and alcohol seem to provide a sense of relaxation after a long day. Many people rely on these substances to unwind and destress. However, it's essential to reflect on how exactly they help us relax.

Imagine giving an infant or a pet pizza, chips, and a beer or a glass of white wine to relax after a long day—it's unthinkable. We instinctively treat them with deep care and respect, preparing healthy meals or selecting the best grain-free food to safeguard their health. Yet, for some reason, we do not extend the same consideration to ourselves. So why do we choose to potentially damage our own bodies and minds with substances that we wouldn't give to those we care about?

The answer is clear: it's due to the addictive nature of alcohol and junk food. They create a cycle where you feel compelled to consume them just to feel relaxed or satisfied. This dependency can lead to obsessive thoughts and behaviors, constantly seeking your next "fix" to alleviate withdrawal symptoms and achieve a temporary sense of well-being.

What worsens this cycle is the physiological and psychological response to these cravings. Sugar and alcohol trigger pleasure centers in the brain, initially providing relief but eventually heightening feelings of stress and unease as their effects wear off. This ongoing cycle perpetuates a state of dependency that negatively impacts both physical health and mental well-being.

In reality, these substances do not actually help you relax. They are the ones creating that feeling of unease, stress, and nervousness in the first place! They temporarily mask stress and anxiety, only to exacerbate these feelings in the long run. The very act of craving and withdrawing from these substances can create a state of nervousness and unease, perpetuating a cycle of dependency.

Imagine a different scenario where you're genuinely healthy and balanced. You wouldn't need these substances to relax because you'd already feel calm and at ease naturally. Your meals would nourish you, leaving you satisfied and content without the need for addictive stimulants. You'd experience genuine relaxation and well-being, free from the ups and downs of dependency.

When you're addicted to junk food, sugar, alcohol, and other substances like these, you only find relief when you consume them. Then you feel terrible again until you can indulge once more. And the cycle goes on and on.

Ultimately, it's about recognizing this addictive cycle and realizing that you can experience true relaxation and fulfillment without compromising your health.

"I don't have time to cook healthy meals, so I rely on fast food."

We've all been there—the end of a long day, exhaustion setting in, and the last thing on your mind is spending hours in the kitchen preparing a meal. It's easy to justify grabbing something quick and convenient, like fast food. After all, who has the time or energy for anything else?

But let's hit pause for a moment and really think about what's at stake here. Is the immediate convenience of junk food worth the toll it can take on our health over time? Let's unpack this dilemma.

Firstly, the belief that fast food is our only viable option when time is tight is a misconception. In reality, there are numerous alternatives worth considering. Simple strategies like meal prepping on weekends or choosing healthier options from fast food menus can make a substantial difference. Instead of defaulting to a cheeseburger, why not opt for a poke bowl or a fresh salad? It's about making choices that balance convenience with health.

Moreover, the notion that cooking healthy meals is time-consuming is also misguided. There's a wide array of nutritious recipes that can be whipped up in under 30 minutes with some planning and smart choices. From stir-fries to hearty soups, these meals not only nourish your body but can also be a fun activity. Cooking can be a chance to bond with your partner, involve your kids in learning about healthy eating habits, and instill values like respect for the environment and animals.

More importantly, consider the example you're setting for your children or younger family members. Your relationship with food shapes their attitudes and behaviors towards eating. By prioritizing nutritious meals, you not only invest in your own well-being but also teach valuable lessons about health and self-care. Your choices today influence their habits for years to come.

When children see adults choosing nutritious meals over fast food, they learn that eating well is not just about taste or convenience—it's about respecting their bodies and promoting long-term health. This lesson becomes ingrained in their lifestyle choices, setting them up for healthier futures.

So, next time you're tempted by the ease of fast food, pause and reflect. Think about the long-term impact on your health and the message it sends to those around you. Embrace the power of making choices that prioritize both convenience and well-being. It's not just about a quick meal—it's about investing in a healthier, happier future for yourself and those you care about.

By making conscious decisions to cook nutritious meals or choose healthier options, you're taking proactive steps towards better health outcomes. You're not only nourishing your body with essential nutrients but also fostering a positive relationship with food that supports overall well-being.

"I've tried diets in the past, but they never work for me long-term."

I hear you. Many diets promise quick fixes and impose rigid restrictions that often lead to feelings of unhappiness, frustration and rebound effects. But what if there's another way—an approach that doesn't demand strict self-control or special diets? It begins with a shift in perspective.

Consider this: what if your relationship with junk food isn't about enjoyment but addiction? For years, you genuinely believed it tasted good and provided relaxation. Now, you're starting to awaken to the truth. You recognize that the fleeting pleasure from junk food masks deeper issues, trapping you in a cycle of craving and regret.

Freeing yourself from this cycle isn't about willpower; it's about awareness and making deliberate choices. Once you realize that you've been conditioned to enjoy something that you actually don't, something that, in fact, harms you, liberation follows naturally. It's empowering to know you can reclaim control over your choices and habits without struggling with diets or succumbing to cravings.

Imagine the boundless energy and vitality you could have if your diet focused on nourishing foods rather than those that drain your energy and cause fatigue. Envision feeling rejuvenated and empowered daily, free from the highs and crashes of junk food.

Do you feel in control of your food choices, or do you often yield to cravings? Picture the satisfaction of regaining command over your eating habits, making decisions that genuinely enhance your well-being.

Have you noticed any patterns between your mood swings and junk food consumption? Consider how junk food affects your mental clarity and overall happiness. Breaking free means reclaiming not just physical health but mental well-being too.

Stop rationalizing and take responsibility. Your choices today shape your life tomorrow. What kind of life do you truly aspire to live? Embrace the power of your choices to create a future that's healthier and happier.

Ultimately, it's about realizing your ability to redefine your relationship with food. It's not about sacrificing pleasure but discovering a new satisfaction—one that nurtures your body and mind for the long term. Are you ready to break free and live a life where your choices empower you?

Junk Food's Impact on Innocence: A Stark Reality

Imagine cradling a newborn in your arms, their innocence a beacon of purity and vulnerability. You gaze into their trusting eyes, feeling the weight of responsibility to nourish them right. Now, picture handing that precious child a cheeseburger dripping with processed cheese and greasy fries swimming in oil, paired with a frothy beer. The scene clashes with everything we instinctively know about nurturing.

Those fries, so oily they leave slicks on your fingers, promise a salty, instant hit that's addictively empty. The cheeseburger, more a chemical creation than food, boasts more preservatives than nutrients. And that beer, all fizz and bitterness, whispers of a culture where junk trumps health.

Imagine this innocent child, craving the fast-food fix. It's not just about taste—it's about a future shaped by quick fixes over real nourishment. Offering this meal isn't just a choice; it's a statement about our values, our priorities, and our kids' wellbeing.

In this contrast lies a stark truth about our times: we're hooked on convenience, trading long-term health for short-lived pleasure. But as we hold that newborn, we hold the future, too. Let's choose nourishment that nurtures, setting a foundation for vitality and strength, not a cycle of empty calories and compromised health.

Brain Manipulation: The Science of Food Addiction

Understanding the mechanics of food addiction involves delving into the complex interplay between our brains and the food we consume. This isn't merely a matter of poor willpower or bad habits; it's a scientifically rooted phenomenon where certain foods manipulate our brain chemistry, leading to addictive behaviors.

Our brains are hardwired to seek pleasure and avoid pain. This basic survival mechanism is governed by the reward system, a network of brain regions that respond to rewarding stimuli by releasing dopamine, the "feel-good" neurotransmitter. Foods high in sugar, fat, and salt are particularly potent in triggering this reward system. When we consume these foods, our brain releases a surge of dopamine, creating a powerful feeling of pleasure and satisfaction. Over time, the brain begins to associate these foods with pleasure, reinforcing the desire to consume them repeatedly. This is similar to the way addictive drugs affect the brain. The more frequently these foods are consumed, the stronger the neural pathways become, making it increasingly difficult to resist the urge to eat them.

Highly processed foods are engineered to be hyper-palatable, meaning they are designed to be irresistibly tasty. This is not accidental; food manufacturers invest heavily in research to find the "bliss point" of their products—the perfect combination of sugar, fat, and salt that maximizes pleasure. When these hyper-palatable foods hijack the brain's reward system, they override natural satiety signals, making it easy to overeat. This can lead to a cycle of binge eating followed by guilt and more cravings, perpetuating the addiction.

Dopamine is central to the cycle of food addiction. With repeated exposure to hyper-palatable foods, the brain becomes less sensitive to dopamine. This means that over time, the same amount of food produces a weaker pleasure response, driving individuals to consume even more to achieve the same level of satisfaction. This process is known as tolerance, a hallmark of addiction. As tolerance develops, the brain also becomes more responsive to cues associated with food, such as the sight, smell, or even the thought of eating. These cues can trigger intense cravings, making it difficult to focus on anything else until the craving is satisfied.

Understanding the science of food addiction highlights that overcoming it is not about sheer willpower but about retraining the brain. Food addiction is a real, scientifically-backed phenomenon that affects millions of people. It's not about lack of discipline but about the intricate ways our brains respond to certain foods. Recognizing that food addiction is a manipulation of the brain's natural reward system is empowering. It shifts the perspective from self-blame to understanding, allowing individuals to take proactive steps toward reclaiming their health. By becoming aware of how certain foods affect the brain, it becomes possible to make more informed choices and break free from the cycle of addiction.

Understanding Evolutionary Aspects

Over millions of years of evolution, human beings developed intricate physiological and metabolic systems that adapted to the natural environment and food availability. Our ancestors' diets were primarily shaped by the availability of wild plants, game meat, and seasonal fruits. This diet provided essential nutrients, fiber, and varied sources of energy.

However, in a remarkably short period—just a few centuries, which is a tiny fraction of the millions of years of human evolution—our eating habits have dramatically changed. The agricultural revolution, beginning around 10,000 years ago, marked a significant shift from hunting and gathering to settled farming communities. This transition introduced grains, dairy products, and cultivated fruits and vegetables into the human diet.

The Industrial Revolution, starting in the late 18th century, accelerated the pace of change. Advances in transportation, food processing, and preservation technologies enabled the mass production and distribution of refined sugars, vegetable oils, and processed foods. This marked the beginning of a profound shift towards a diet high in refined carbohydrates, added sugars, unhealthy fats, and artificial additives.

In the span of just a few hundred years, human diets have shifted from natural, whole foods to highly processed, calorie-dense products that are often low in essential nutrients. This rapid change has disrupted the delicate balance of our evolutionary adaptations. Our bodies, finely tuned over millennia to efficiently process natural foods, now struggle to cope with the excesses of modern diets.

Understanding these evolutionary aspects of feeding and living habits provides crucial insights into why modern humans have certain food preferences and behaviors. By examining how early humans fed and lived, we can better understand the roots of our dietary inclinations.

Early humans were primarily hunters and gatherers. Their survival depended on their ability to find and consume food in an environment where availability was unpredictable. They foraged for fruits, nuts, roots, and other plant materials while hunting animals for meat. This lifestyle was marked by irregular access to food sources. During times of abundance, early humans would consume as much as possible to build energy reserves, storing excess calories as body fat. This fat storage was crucial for surviving periods of scarcity, particularly during the harsh winters when food was scarce. Animals exhibit similar survival strategies. For instance, bears eat excessively before hibernation, accumulating fat to sustain them through the winter months.

Migratory birds also eat intensively before long flights, ensuring they have enough energy for their journey. These behaviors highlight a fundamental survival mechanism: maximizing energy intake when food is available to endure periods when it is not.

Our evolutionary history has shaped not only our feeding habits but also our taste preferences. Early humans evolved to crave sugar and fat. These tastes were associated with foods that provided essential energy and nutrients. Sweet foods, such as fruits, were rich in quick energy and generally safe to eat, making them a desirable food source. Fats offered a dense form of long-lasting energy, essential for survival during lean times. These preferences ensured that early humans selected the most energy-rich and nutritionally beneficial foods available.

However, unlike today, early humans did not have regular access to salt. Natural salt sources were rare and sporadically available, meaning that our bodies are not evolved to handle the high levels of salt found in modern diets. Excessive salt consumption today contributes to numerous health problems, including hypertension and heart disease.

In the modern world, the abundance of processed foods, engineered to be hyper-palatable and high in sugar, fat, and salt, exploits our natural inclinations. This often results in overeating and related health issues, such as obesity and diabetes. The evolutionary adaptations that once favored survival now clash with our current food environment, posing significant challenges to maintaining a healthy diet.

In addition to our cravings for certain tastes, our eating habits have also dramatically changed. For example, consider the common practice of drinking a glass of orange juice in the morning. To make one glass of orange juice, you need approximately four oranges. Realistically, very few people would sit down and eat four whole oranges in one sitting. Consuming the fruit in its whole form would provide natural fiber, helping to regulate the body's sugar absorption and create a feeling of fullness.

However, when we drink orange juice, we consume the concentrated sugar and calories of multiple oranges without the fiber, leading to a rapid spike in blood sugar levels. This can contribute to overconsumption of calories and may cause various health issues, such as weight gain, insulin resistance, and an increased risk of developing type 2 diabetes. The fiber in whole fruit slows down the digestive process, leading to a more gradual release of sugar into the bloodstream. This not only helps maintain steady energy levels but also supports better metabolic health.

Also, our modern eating habits often involve consuming a variety of foods in combinations that would have been uncommon for our ancestors. In the past, meals were simpler and typically consisted of a single type of food at a time. Early humans might have had a meal of just hunted meat or gathered fruits and nuts, but not a mix of meats, vegetables, fruits, cheese, wine and desserts all in one sitting. Our digestive systems evolved to handle these simpler meals, processing one type of aliment at a time efficiently.

Today, however, our meals are often a complex mix of different food types. For instance, a typical modern meal might include a steak (protein and fat), a salad with various vegetables, a carbohydrate source like bread or pasta, and a dessert rich in sugars and fats. This combination requires our digestive system to work harder and manage the breakdown of diverse nutrients simultaneously. Our stomachs are not designed to digest such a variety of foods at once, which can lead to digestive issues such as bloating, indigestion, and nutrient malabsorption.

Consider eating meat, eggs, or fish two or three times a day—does that sound natural to you? Our ancient ancestors certainly didn't indulge in such regular feasts. They lived in sync with nature's rhythms, relying on sporadic hunting, gathering, or fishing for these prized protein sources. Their diets were shaped by scarcity and abundance, fostering a diverse intake of foods that varied with the seasons and environmental conditions.

Our drinking habits today diverge drastically from our natural dietary patterns. Early humans thrived on water; their bodies perfectly adapted to this pure, essential source of hydration. It was simple, effective, and crucial for their survival. Fast forward to modern times, and our beverage choices have exploded—sugary drinks, milk, coffee, alcohol—they're everywhere. These options flood our diets with unnecessary calories and disrupt the delicate balance of hydration our bodies crave. Sugary drinks cause rapid spikes in blood sugar, leaving us parched and craving more. Alcohol can dehydrate us faster than we realize, affecting our body's ability to function at its best. By straying from nature's intended hydration solution, we invite a host of health issues that early humans never had to contend with. It's time to rethink our drinks and get back to basics with what our bodies truly need: water.

The convenience and availability of processed foods have further exacerbated these issues. Many processed foods are designed to be hyper-palatable, combining high levels of sugar, fat, and salt to make them more appealing. This combination is rare in natural foods and was not something our ancestors encountered. As a result, these modern foods can easily lead to overconsumption, as they trigger pleasure centers in the brain more intensely than whole foods do.

The Ancient Practice of Fasting

Another significant aspect of early human diets was the necessity of fasting during periods when food was not available. This was particularly evident during winter months when resources were scarce, and hunting or gathering could be challenging. Early humans often went long periods without eating, a stark contrast to our current era of abundant and readily available food.

Intermittent fasting, as practiced by our ancestors out of necessity, played a crucial role in regulating metabolism and maintaining a healthy balance of body weight and energy reserves. During these fasting periods, the body would switch from using glucose as its primary energy source to breaking down stored fats into ketones for energy. This metabolic flexibility allowed early humans to survive and function optimally even in times of food scarcity.

Modern nutritional science is increasingly recognizing the benefits of fasting. Research has shown that intermittent fasting can improve various aspects of metabolic health, including insulin sensitivity, cholesterol levels, and blood pressure. By allowing the body to enter a state of autophagy—a process where cells break down and recycle damaged components—fasting can also contribute to cellular repair and longevity. This cellular "housekeeping" is essential for maintaining healthy tissues and organs and may reduce the risk of chronic diseases such as cancer and Alzheimer's.

Additionally, fasting can help with weight management. In the absence of a constant food supply, the body naturally uses stored fat for energy, leading to a reduction in body fat. This is particularly beneficial in today's context, where obesity and related metabolic disorders are prevalent due to continuous access to calorie-dense foods.

The benefits of fasting extend beyond physical health to mental clarity and cognitive function. Historical accounts suggest that early humans experienced heightened mental acuity during periods of fasting, likely an evolutionary adaptation to aid in finding food. Modern studies support this, indicating that intermittent fasting can enhance brain function and protect against neurodegenerative diseases. The brain's response to fasting includes improved synaptic plasticity, increased production of neurotrophic factors, and enhanced stress resistance.

Moreover, fasting has psychological benefits. In a society where food is often consumed not just for nourishment but also for comfort and stress relief, periodic fasting can help reset our relationship with food. It promotes mindfulness and helps individuals distinguish between true hunger and habitual eating patterns driven by external cues or emotions.

In addition to these individual benefits, fasting can also have a positive impact on the environment. Reduced food consumption means lower demand for agricultural production, which can decrease the strain on natural resources and reduce greenhouse gas emissions. Historically, the natural ebb and flow of food availability helped maintain ecological balance, a principle that holds relevance in the context of modern sustainability efforts.

Furthermore, intermittent fasting aligns with the natural rhythms of our biology. The circadian rhythm, which governs our sleep-wake cycle, also influences our digestive processes. Eating in alignment with our circadian rhythm—having meals during daylight hours and fasting during the night— can optimize digestion and nutrient absorption, enhance metabolic health, and improve sleep quality.

How Does the Addiction Work

Food addiction is a complex interplay involving our body, mind, and environment. It intertwines neural pathways, emotional triggers, and societal influences, shaping our cravings and consumption habits.

Imagine your brain as a bustling city where neurotransmitters are like busy messengers darting between towering skyscrapers of neurons. When you consume foods rich in sugar, fat, or salt, these substances swiftly infiltrate your brain's command center, hijacking its reward system. Dopamine, the brain's key pleasure and reward neurotransmitter, floods the streets, creating a euphoric rush that amplifies the desire for more.

Just as a city buzzes with excitement during a festival, your brain lights up with pleasure signals from dopamine, reinforcing the craving for these hyper-palatable foods. This biochemical phenomenon is akin to turning up the volume on a favorite song, making each bite or sip intensely satisfying. Over time, this repeated exposure rewires the brain, altering its chemistry and structure. The once subtle pleasures of natural foods are overshadowed by the intense allure of processed delights, leading to a heightened appetite and a drive to seek out more.

In this neural cityscape, the dopamine surge is like a dazzling fireworks display, captivating your brain and fueling the desire to consume these foods despite knowing their potential harm. It's a complex interplay of biology and behavior, where the brain's reward pathways adapt to prioritize the pursuit of pleasure, sometimes at the expense of long-term health and well-being.

Repeated exposure to hyper-palatable foods, rich in sugar, fat, or salt, gradually modifies the brain's chemistry and structure. Initially, these foods simply trigger a surge in dopamine, creating a euphoric sensation. However, over time, the brain adapts to this constant stimulation by desensitizing its reward pathways. This desensitization means that greater quantities of these foods are needed to achieve the same level of satisfaction as before, similar to how drug tolerance develops in substance addiction. As a result, individuals may find themselves consuming larger portions or seeking out more intensely flavored foods to experience the same pleasure they once did with smaller amounts. This cycle reinforces the addictive behavior, making it challenging to break free from the grip of food cravings and overconsumption.

Beyond its biochemical effects, food addiction deeply intertwines with our emotional and psychological realms. Various emotional states such as stress, loneliness, boredom, and even happiness can trigger intense cravings for certain foods. These cravings often serve as coping mechanisms, seemingly providing comfort or distraction during emotional highs and lows. Over time, these emotional cues become deeply embedded in our eating habits, forming strong associations that drive compulsive behaviors.

For instance, stress may prompt us to reach for sugary snacks or comfort foods as a way to alleviate tension or anxiety. Loneliness might lead to seeking solace in food, filling an emotional void with the temporary pleasure of eating. Boredom can trigger mindless eating, where food becomes a way to pass the time or provide entertainment. Even happiness can be linked to food, with celebrations and social gatherings often centered around indulgent meals or desserts.

These emotional triggers reinforce the association between food and mood regulation. As we repeatedly turn to food for emotional comfort or reward, neural pathways in the brain strengthen, solidifying the link between specific emotions and eating behaviors. This intertwining of emotions and eating habits can lead to a cycle of compulsive eating, where food becomes a primary means of coping with and regulating emotional experiences. Recognizing and addressing these emotional triggers is crucial in overcoming food addiction and establishing healthier relationships with food and emotions alike.

After consuming foods high in sugar, the initial rush of dopamine creates a temporary euphoric sensation, often described as a "sugar high." However, this surge is short-lived, followed by a crash that can leave us feeling low, sad, anxious, or even depressed. This rollercoaster of highs and lows is an addictive cycle, where the need for more sugar arises to achieve that initial high again.

Ironically, while food is sought as solace from life's stresses, it is actually what often perpetuates these emotional fluctuations. The sugar rush artificially boosts mood, masking underlying emotions temporarily. When the effects wear off, the crash intensifies negative feelings, prompting a renewed craving for more sugar to alleviate discomfort.

This cycle creates a deceptive pattern where food appears to soothe emotional distress but ultimately exacerbates it. Rather than addressing the root causes of stress or emotional discomfort, reliance on sugary foods perpetuates a cycle of dependence and fluctuating moods. Understanding this dynamic is crucial for recognizing that food, particularly foods high in sugar, isn't a true solution but rather a contributor to emotional instability and dependency.

In our modern environment, the challenge intensifies. Indeed today's world, food surrounds us everywhere we go. It's not just abundant and convenient; it's aggressively marketed, enticing us with promises of pleasure and fulfillment at every turn. Fast food chains beckon with their convenience, offering quick fixes for hunger without the hassle of preparation. Meanwhile, sugary snacks promise immediate satisfaction, tapping into our desire for instant gratification.

Advertisements bombard us with images of delicious meals, decadent desserts, and tempting treats, presenting food as a source of comfort, reward, and happiness. This constant exposure to food messaging normalizes overconsumption and reinforces addictive eating patterns. It creates a culture where indulgence is celebrated and moderation feels like an unattainable ideal.

In this environment, resisting the urge to overeat or choose unhealthy options becomes a monumental challenge. The pervasive availability and relentless marketing of hyper-palatable foods make it easy to fall into patterns of excessive consumption. What starts as a craving can quickly escalate into a habit, driven by the belief that food provides solace or distraction from daily stresses.

Once we awaken to the truth that what we consume can be a silent poison, gradually undermining our vitality and well-being, breaking free from these influences becomes remarkably straightforward. It's about confronting our relationship with food directly, understanding the profound psychological and social triggers behind our cravings, and consciously prioritizing long-term vitality over fleeting satisfaction. By rejecting the pervasive culture of excess and embracing mindful moderation, we effortlessly regain control over our eating habits.

Strategies to Break the Cycle of Addiction and Regain Control

Start by questioning everything you thought you knew about food and nutrition. Dive deep into how junk food exploits your brain's reward system, fostering insatiable cravings that undermine your health and well-being. It's crucial to confront the uncomfortable truth: your addiction to these foods is a significant barrier holding you back from realizing your full potential and living a vibrant life. Are you truly ready to break free and thrive?

Consider this: junk food and alcohol industries capitalize on your addiction, meticulously crafting flavors and formulations designed to keep you hooked. They profit from your vulnerability, perpetuating a cycle of dependence that masks deeper emotional and psychological needs. Ask yourself: are you comfortable allowing these corporations to control your choices and health?

Recognize that your dependence on junk food and alcohol isn't just a habit—it's a form of self-sabotage. What fears or aspirations might you be avoiding by turning to these substances for comfort or distraction? By confronting these underlying motivations, you can begin to dismantle the grip they have on your life and open pathways to genuine fulfillment and growth.

Breaking free from food and alcohol addiction isn't about willpower; it's about reclaiming control over your choices and forging a new relationship with nourishment and self-care. For many years, junk food and alcohol seemed like a delicious, comforting, relaxing crutch—a tempting indulgence you couldn't resist. It felt like you could never stop eating these foods or drinking wine and beer because you genuinely believed they brought you pleasure and relaxation. However, now you see it was all an illusion carefully designed by the food industry to manipulate your cravings. In reality, these substances are poison, wreaking havoc on your veins, vital organs, and mental health.

Now that you've awakened to this truth, you are liberated. You don't need a special strategy or complex plan to overcome addiction. Simply knowing the reality behind their allure is enough. You are free from their grip and now have the power to master your own life and health.

With this newfound awareness, you embark on a transformative journey where you can now confidently provide yourself and your family with wholesome, nourishing meals. No longer enslaved by the cravings and allure of junk food, you understand that these harmful substances have no place in your kitchen or your loved ones' bodies. Breaking free from this addiction isn't just about personal liberation; it's about setting a powerful example and fostering a culture of wellness within your home.

Imagine the satisfaction of preparing meals that fuel both body and soul, knowing every ingredient contributes to your family's vitality and well-being. Embracing a diet rich in whole foods, fruits, vegetables, and lean proteins becomes not just a choice but a joyful celebration of health. Your newfound clarity allows you to prioritize nutritious options without sacrificing flavor or satisfaction.

Do you want to be the reason why your children struggle with health issues linked to poor diet choices? Picture the impact of your decision to prioritize their well-being by offering them nutritious meals instead of processed junk. You have the power to shape their future health outcomes by instilling healthy eating habits from an early age. It's a responsibility that transcends mealtime—it's a legacy of vitality and resilience that you can proudly pass down to generations.

Breaking free from junk food addiction opens doors to a brighter, healthier future for you and your family. It's about reclaiming control over your life, making informed choices that promote longevity and vitality. Imagine the peace of mind knowing that your family is nourished in a way that supports their growth, development, and overall health. By embracing this journey, you pave the way for a life where wellness and joy go hand in hand, free from the shackles of food addiction.

Sugar's Mental Maze: Unraveling the Impact on Clarity

Imagine your brain as a bustling cityscape, where neurons are busy streets and synapses are the bridges connecting thoughts and actions. Now, envision sugar as a mischievous maze that suddenly materializes within this vibrant city.

At first, sugar's presence seems innocuous, like playful twists and turns that promise fleeting excitement. However, as you venture deeper into the maze, the path becomes convoluted and uncertain. Neurons misfire, struggling to navigate the erratic twists and turns imposed by sugar's chaotic design.

Picture sugar as a trickster, leading your thoughts astray with false promises of energy and pleasure. It disrupts the smooth flow of neurotransmitters, causing signals to misinterpret and leaving your mental cityscape in disarray. Like a labyrinth of confusion, this interference can manifest as mood swings, anxiety, and difficulty concentrating.

Moreover, sugar's impact extends beyond momentary confusion. Continued consumption can build walls within the maze, obstructing clear pathways for information processing and memory retrieval. It's like trying to find your way through a foggy labyrinth where clarity and coherence are obscured by sugar's intricate traps.

As you navigate this mental maze, it's essential to tread carefully. Choose nourishment that supports the cityscape of your brain—foods rich in nutrients like antioxidants and omega-3 fatty acids that promote clarity and resilience. By steering clear of sugar's maze and embracing a diet that nurtures mental clarity, you empower your brain to thrive amidst the twists and turns of daily life.

Managing Withdrawal Symptoms

Navigating junk food withdrawal marks a pivotal step towards reclaiming your health and well-being. As you embark on this journey, it's essential to recognize that eliminating junk food from your diet can trigger a range of physical and psychological symptoms akin to those experienced in other forms of addiction. These symptoms—irritability, mood swings, headaches, fatigue—signal that your body is undergoing a profound transformation. Typically, they peak in the initial days after reducing junk food intake due to the abrupt change in diet and the body's reaction to withdrawal from additives like sugars, artificial flavorings, and excessive fats. The intensity and duration of these symptoms may vary depending on factors such as individual metabolism, overall health, and previous dietary habits.

During this period, the brain and body are adjusting to the absence of these stimulants, which previously provided quick bursts of energy and pleasure. The sudden reduction in these substances can disrupt neurotransmitter levels, particularly dopamine, leading to mood instability and heightened sensitivity to stressors.

Physiologically, headaches may occur as the body adjusts to fluctuating blood sugar levels and the absence of additives like MSG. Fatigue often accompanies this adjustment phase as the body shifts from relying on processed foods for energy to metabolizing nutrient-dense alternatives more efficiently.

Experiencing withdrawal symptoms when eliminating junk food from your diet is a clear sign that positive change is underway. These symptoms indicate that your body is detoxifying and adjusting to healthier eating habits. Rather than viewing these symptoms as obstacles, consider them as milestones of progress—a testament to your determination to break free from food addiction and improve your well-being.

Each symptom you encounter signifies that your body was accustomed to the artificial stimulation provided by junk food. Feeling irritable or experiencing intense cravings means your brain is recalibrating its response to food cues, moving away from the immediate gratification of processed foods towards the sustainable nourishment of whole foods. Every discomfort you feel is a reminder of your commitment to change and a step closer to achieving lasting health benefits.

Embracing these symptoms as victories rather than painful moments can shift your perspective and empower you on your journey. Celebrate each headache or mood swing as a sign that your body is purging itself of toxins and resetting its natural balance. Recognize that the more intense these symptoms, the deeper your reliance on junk food may have been—and the more profound your progress towards liberation from its grip.

By reframing these challenges as positive indicators of transformation, you can cultivate resilience and perseverance throughout the withdrawal process. Remember, feeling these symptoms means your body is working to shed its dependency on unhealthy foods. With each passing day, your resilience will grow, and your body and mind will align more closely with your goal of vibrant health and well-being.

Managing irritability, mood swings, headaches, and fatigue during the transition away from junk food can be effectively handled with several straightforward strategies.

Firstly, staying adequately hydrated is crucial. Dehydration can exacerbate symptoms such as headaches and fatigue. Make sure to drink enough water throughout the day to support your body's detoxification processes.

Regular and balanced meals play a vital role in stabilizing blood sugar levels. Focus on consuming whole foods like fruits, vegetables, lean proteins, and whole grains. These foods provide sustained energy and help prevent mood swings and irritability.

Including nutrient-dense foods in your diet is also essential. Foods rich in vitamins and minerals can alleviate symptoms and support your overall health. For instance, foods high in magnesium, such as nuts, seeds, and leafy greens, are beneficial for managing headaches and promoting mood stability.

Ensuring adequate sleep is also crucial for managing fatigue. Establish a regular sleep schedule and practice good sleep hygiene to support your body's recovery and energy levels.

Incorporating regular physical activity into your routine can boost mood and energy levels while reducing symptoms of withdrawal. Find activities you enjoy and make them a part of your daily life.

Lastly, seek support from friends, family, or a healthcare professional who can provide encouragement and guidance throughout your journey. Sharing your experience with others who understand can make the transition smoother and more manageable.

By implementing these strategies consistently and with patience, you can effectively manage irritability, mood swings, headaches, and fatigue as your body adapts to a healthier diet and lifestyle.

The Grip of Temptation: Unraveling Junk Food Addiction

Imagine junk food as a seductive sirens' song, echoing through the corridors of your mind with irresistible allure. It begins innocently enough, a fleeting taste that ignites pleasure centers in your brain like twinkling lights in the night sky. Yet, with each indulgence, the melody grows louder, weaving its way into the fabric of your cravings.

The initial taste is a gentle tug, a whisper of satisfaction that promises instant gratification. Picture it as a tantalizing aroma that lingers in the air, teasing your senses and inviting you closer. As you succumb to its allure, the flavors explode on your palate like fireworks, releasing a rush of dopamine that momentarily soothes stress and fatigue.

Yet, beneath the surface, this seductive whisper conceals a potent allure that grows stronger with each indulgence. It's a beguiling melody that reverberates through your thoughts, weaving a web of cravings that demand to be satisfied. The more you heed its call, the louder it resonates, becoming a constant presence in your mind's symphony.

This relentless allure of junk food is like a spellbinding enchantress, casting a hypnotic spell over your desires. It promises pleasure and comfort, but its grip tightens with every bite, ensnaring you in a cycle of craving and indulgence. What begins as a fleeting taste evolves into a symphony of cravings that dominate your thoughts and influence your choices.

Junk food emerges as a seductive force—a siren's song that captivates with promises of pleasure and ease. Yet, beneath its alluring facade lies a cycle of dependency that clouds judgment and challenges self-control. Recognizing this allure empowers you to navigate its temptations with mindfulness and make choices that prioritize long-term health and well-being.

Cultivating Health: A Comprehensive Plan

Our health often takes a backseat to convenience and instant gratification. Yet, deep down, we know that true vitality and well-being stem from nurturing our bodies with wholesome nutrition and mindful practices. This journey begins with a fundamental shift in how we approach food—detoxifying ourselves from the grip of junk food and embracing a lifestyle that cultivates lasting health.

Detoxifying from junk food isn't about cutting calories or shedding pounds; it's about reclaiming control over what fuels our bodies. Junk foods, laden with sugars, unhealthy fats, and artificial additives, hijack our taste buds and trigger addictive responses in our brains. They promise fleeting pleasure but leave us drained, sluggish, and craving more. Recognizing these foods for what they are—empty promises—is the first step towards liberation.

Cultivating health means understanding the profound impact of our food choices beyond immediate satisfaction. It means recognizing the difference between bad and good foods—those rich in essential nutrients, antioxidants, and beneficial compounds that support our immune system, enhance cognitive function, and promote overall vitality. It's about embracing foods that nourish our cells deeply, rather than simply fill us up.

Recognizing Healthy Foods

Healthy foods encompass a diverse range of options rich in vitamins, minerals, fiber, and antioxidants. These include fresh fruits, vegetables, lean proteins, whole grains, nuts, seeds, and legumes, all crucial for supporting optimal bodily function and well-being.

Choose foods that are minimally processed or close to their natural state. Aim for a variety of colorful options, as different colors often signify a variety of vitamins, minerals, and antioxidants.

Fresh Fruits and Vegetables: Fresh fruits and vegetables are not just essential components of a healthy diet; they are vibrant expressions of nature's bounty, offering an unparalleled spectrum of nutrients that nourish and sustain our bodies. Take oranges, for example. With their bright, citrusy hues and juicy flesh, they are not only a delight to the senses but also a powerhouse of vitamin C. This nutrient supports our immune system, helping us ward off illnesses and infections, but also plays a crucial role in collagen production, keeping our skin youthful and resilient against environmental stressors.

Leafy greens like spinach and kale are verdant symbols of vitality in the culinary world. Picture a bunch of fresh spinach, its deep green leaves glistening with dew-like droplets, packed with vitamins A, C, and K. These nutrients are not just names on a label; they are the building blocks of our health. Vitamin A supports our vision and skin health, vitamin C boosts our immune defenses, and vitamin K ensures our blood clots properly and supports bone health. Together with folate and iron found abundantly in spinach, these nutrients contribute to our energy levels, red blood cell production, and overall well-being. Kale brims with vitamins A, C, and K, minerals like manganese and copper, and an arsenal of antioxidants. These antioxidants act as our body's defenders, scavenging harmful free radicals that can damage our cells and contribute to chronic diseases. Manganese supports our bones and metabolism, while copper facilitates iron absorption and strengthens our connective tissues, ensuring we stay agile and resilient.

Colorful fruits and vegetables, from the deep purples of blueberries to the vibrant reds of bell peppers and the sunny yellows of sweet potatoes, offer more than just visual appeal. They are nature's pharmacy, brimming with phytochemicals and antioxidants that promote cellular health and longevity. Berries are packed with anthocyanins, potent antioxidants that help reduce inflammation and protect our cardiovascular system. Bell peppers, with their crisp texture and vibrant colors, are not just versatile in the kitchen; they are rich sources of vitamins A and C, which support our immune system, vision, and skin health. Meanwhile, sweet potatoes, with their earthy sweetness and creamy flesh, provide a wealth of beta-carotene, an antioxidant that our bodies convert into vitamin A for healthy eyes and skin.

Lean Proteins: Lean proteins stand as pillars of strength and sustenance in our quest for optimal health and vitality. Picture a tender chicken breast, grilled to perfection, its savory aroma wafting through the kitchen. This lean cut not only satisfies our hunger but also provides high-quality protein essential for muscle growth, repair, and maintenance. Unlike processed meats laden with saturated fats that weigh us down, chicken breast offers lean nourishment that supports our body's natural strength and resilience.

Tofu, a versatile plant-based protein, embodies a different kind of strength in its smooth texture and ability to absorb flavors. Imagine cubes of tofu sizzling in a stir-fry, soaking up the savory sauces and spices. This plant-based protein powerhouse not only supports muscle growth but also provides a complete source of essential amino acids necessary for our body's repair processes. Tofu is a testament to the diversity of protein sources available to us, offering a sustainable and nutritious alternative to animal-based proteins.

Salmon offers more than just a delectable meal. Omega-3 fatty acids found abundantly in salmon support cardiovascular health by reducing inflammation and improving cholesterol levels. Additionally, these essential fats promote brain function and cognitive health, ensuring clarity and focus throughout our day.

Legumes such as lentils and chickpeas are hearty champions in the realm of plant-based proteins. Imagine a warm bowl of lentil soup, its earthy aroma inviting comfort and nourishment. Lentils are not only rich in protein but also provide a wealth of fiber, iron, and magnesium—essential minerals that support energy production, muscle function, and overall vitality. Meanwhile, chickpeas, whether roasted for a crunchy snack or blended into creamy hummus, offer a nutritious boost of protein and fiber that satisfies hunger while stabilizing blood sugar levels.

Whole Grains: Whole grains stand as stalwarts of nutrition, their wholesome goodness woven into the fabric of a balanced diet. Oats, revered for their fiber content, not only promote digestive health but also provide a steady release of energy that sustains us throughout the day. Unlike refined grains stripped of their nutrient-rich layers, oats retain their bran and germ, ensuring we receive the full spectrum of B vitamins and minerals like magnesium and selenium that support overall vitality.

Quinoa, an ancient grain celebrated for its complete protein profile and delicate texture, paints a picture of culinary versatility. Picture a colorful quinoa salad, its grains a mosaic of red, white, and black, complemented by vibrant vegetables and a zesty dressing. Quinoa stands out among grains for its ability to nourish us with essential amino acids necessary for muscle repair and growth. Its complex carbohydrates provide sustained energy, making it a favored choice for athletes and health-conscious individuals alike seeking endurance and satiety.

Brown rice, with its nutty flavor and chewy texture, supports digestive health by promoting regularity and preventing spikes in blood sugar levels. Its magnesium content aids in muscle function and relaxation, contributing to overall well-being and vitality.

Whole wheat, found in hearty breads and pastas, embodies the essence of nourishment with its robust flavor and dense texture. Unlike its refined counterparts, whole wheat retains its fiber-rich bran and germ, offering a multitude of health benefits. From regulating cholesterol levels to reducing the risk of heart disease and type 2 diabetes, whole wheat plays a pivotal role in supporting long-term health and wellness.

Nuts and Seeds: Nuts and seeds emerge as tiny powerhouses of nutrition, offering a treasure trove of health benefits with every crunchy bite. Almonds, rich in vitamin E, magnesium, and antioxidants, stand as guardians of heart health, combating inflammation and supporting overall cardiovascular function. Their natural goodness extends beyond mere snacking, offering a nutrient-packed boost to our daily diet that nourishes both body and mind.

Chia seeds, in contrast, reveal a different kind of nutritional magic with their tiny size and potent benefits. Their omega-3 fatty acids and fiber content promotes satiety and digestive health. These tiny seeds transform simple dishes into nutrient-dense powerhouses, supporting our quest for vitality with every spoonful.

Pumpkin seeds, known for their delicate crunch and earthy flavor, offer yet another glimpse into the diverse world of nuts and seeds. Imagine roasting pumpkin seeds with a hint of sea salt, their satisfying crunch and nutritional profile delivering essential minerals like zinc and magnesium. These seeds, often overlooked but rich in protein, fiber, and healthy fats, provide a nourishing addition to salads, baked goods, or enjoyed straight from the handful.

Flaxseeds, with their mild, nutty taste and versatile nature, contribute to both culinary creativity and nutritional excellence. Celebrated for their high fiber content, they promote digestive regularity and satiety, making them a valued ally in maintaining overall well-being.

Walnuts, with their distinctively rich flavor and texture, round out the spectrum of nuts and seeds with their unique health benefits. Their omega-3 fatty acids and antioxidants support brain health and reduce inflammation, promoting longevity and resilience.

Nourishing the Microbiome

In addition to consuming a diverse range of foods, especially those rich in fiber such as fruits, vegetables, whole grains, and legumes, probiotics and prebiotics play crucial roles in nurturing beneficial gut bacteria.

Probiotics are microscopic champions of gut health, thriving in fermented foods like yogurt, kefir, sauerkraut, and kimchi. They establish themselves in your digestive system, forming a robust community that promotes smooth digestion and bolsters your immune system.

Think of probiotics as beneficial bacteria that settle down in your gut like pioneers in a new territory. They actively work to maintain a balanced microbiota, ensuring that digestion operates efficiently and immune defenses remain strong. By consuming probiotic-rich foods regularly, such as yogurt with Lactobacillus acidophilus or kefir packed with diverse bacterial strains, you introduce these beneficial microorganisms into your gut.

Probiotics play essential roles beyond digestion. They help break down food, produce vitamins, and contribute to the production of short-chain fatty acids, which support gut health and reduce inflammation. Moreover, they interact with your immune system, influencing its responses and potentially enhancing overall immune function.

Including probiotics in your diet can be as simple as incorporating a serving of yogurt or a portion of fermented vegetables like sauerkraut or kimchi into your meals. For those needing a more targeted approach, probiotic supplements offer specific strains in concentrated forms, especially beneficial during periods of stress, illness, or antibiotic use when gut flora may be compromised.

Prebiotics, on the other hand, are dietary fibers that serve as fuel for beneficial gut bacteria, found in foods like garlic, onions, bananas, and whole grains. Unlike probiotics, which are live microorganisms, prebiotics pass through the digestive system intact, reaching the colon where they are fermented by gut bacteria.

Think of prebiotics as the nourishing foundation for your gut ecosystem. They provide essential nutrients that beneficial bacteria like Bifidobacteria and Lactobacilli thrive on, promoting a diverse and balanced microbiota. By including prebiotic-rich foods in your diet, such as fiber-packed vegetables and whole grains, you support the growth and activity of these beneficial bacteria.

The benefits of prebiotics extend beyond digestion. As they ferment in the colon, prebiotics produce short-chain fatty acids like butyrate, which contribute to gut health by supporting the intestinal lining and reducing inflammation. Additionally, they may influence metabolic health, immunity, and even mental well-being through the gut-brain axis.

Incorporating prebiotics into your daily meals can be straightforward. Add slices of raw garlic to dressings, include onions in stir-fries, snack on bananas, or choose whole grains like oats and barley. These dietary choices not only enhance the health of your gut but also contribute to overall wellness by supporting a thriving microbiota and its beneficial effects on various aspects of your health.

Together, probiotics and prebiotics work synergistically with a fiber-rich diet to maintain a diverse and thriving microbiome. By incorporating these elements into your daily nutrition, you support not only digestive health but also overall well-being and immune resilience.

Mindful Eating

Mindful eating is a practice that encourages awareness and intentionality in how we approach food and eating. It involves paying full attention to the sensory experiences, thoughts, and emotions that arise during meals.

By being fully present during meals, mindful eating enhances the enjoyment and satisfaction derived from eating. It promotes a non-judgmental awareness of our eating habits and attitudes towards food, reducing guilt or shame associated with choices.

Tuning in to our body's hunger and fullness signals is a key aspect of mindful eating. This helps us eat when genuinely hungry and stop when comfortably satisfied, fostering a healthier relationship with food and preventing overeating.

Mindful eating also involves recognizing emotional triggers that influence our eating behaviors, encouraging us to find alternative ways to cope with emotions without resorting to food.

Slowing down the pace of eating is another component of mindful eating. This allows us to savor each bite, aids digestion, and helps our body register fullness more effectively, reducing the risk of overeating.

Moreover, mindful eating promotes an appreciation for the origins of our food and the effort involved in its production and preparation. This awareness can deepen our connection to food and cultivate gratitude for nourishing meals.

Benefits of mindful eating include improved digestion through thorough chewing and slower eating, better weight management by responding to hunger cues, reduced stress levels during meals, enhanced satisfaction from food, and improved food choices aligned with health goals.

In essence, mindful eating is about fostering a respectful and attentive relationship with food. It encourages us to eat with awareness, honoring our body's needs and the nourishment that food provides, while promoting overall well-being through healthier eating habits and a positive mindset towards food.

Addressing Common Misconceptions

Healthy Food Tastes Bland: Healthy meals can tantalize the taste buds with vibrant flavors and satisfying textures when crafted with the right ingredients and culinary methods. Incorporating a rich array of herbs and spices not only adds depth and complexity to dishes but also brings potent antioxidants and phytonutrients that support overall health. Meanwhile, incorporating healthy fats—such as those found in avocados, nuts, and olive oil—not only boosts satiety but also provides essential fatty acids crucial for heart health and cognitive function. By skillfully combining these elements, you can create meals that are as nourishing for the body as they are delightful for the palate, proving that eating healthily is a gratifying culinary adventure rather than a sacrifice.

Eating Organic Automatically Means Healthy: Eating organic is often perceived as synonymous with healthier choices due to reduced pesticide exposure. However, it's essential to recognize that organic foods can still contain high levels of sugar, salt, or unhealthy fats if not chosen mindfully. Simply opting for organic does not guarantee a nutritious option. To make informed decisions, reading labels remains crucial.

Dietary Supplements Can Replace a Healthy Diet: While supplements serve a valuable role in addressing nutrient deficiencies, they should not be seen as substitutes for a varied and well-rounded diet that includes whole foods. Supplements are designed to provide concentrated doses of specific nutrients but they do not replicate the complex interactions and synergies found in whole foods, which offer a spectrum of vitamins, minerals, antioxidants, fiber, and other beneficial compounds that support overall health.

Eating Gluten-Free is Always Healthier: Eating gluten-free is often seen as universally healthier, but unless you have celiac disease or gluten intolerance, cutting out gluten may not bring extra health benefits and could lead to nutrient deficiencies if not managed carefully. For those with celiac disease, gluten triggers immune reactions that harm the small intestine, impairing nutrient absorption. However, for most people, gluten-free diets could limit food choices unnecessarily, potentially missing out on vital nutrients found in grains like wheat, barley, and rye, such as fiber, B vitamins, iron, and minerals crucial for health. Many gluten-free products on the market are processed and can be higher in sugar, unhealthy fats, and additives, which might offset any health gains from cutting out gluten. It's crucial to plan a balanced diet that includes gluten-free whole grains like quinoa and brown rice, along with fruits, vegetables, lean proteins, and dairy, ensuring nutritional needs are met without unnecessary restrictions.

Smoothies are Healthy: Smoothies are often touted as a healthy choice, but the reality is nuanced. While homemade versions using whole fruits and vegetables can indeed be nutritious, many store-bought options are loaded with added sugars and lack sufficient fiber. These factors can counteract the potential health benefits of the ingredients. Opting for homemade smoothies allows control over the ingredients, ensuring they are packed with nutrients and free from unnecessary additives. When selecting store-bought options, it's crucial to scrutinize labels and choose products with minimal added sugars and high fiber content to maximize their nutritional value.

Eating Healthy Means Never Eating Out: Eating healthy doesn't mean you have to avoid dining out altogether. It's entirely possible to make smart, nutritious choices when eating at restaurants. By opting for grilled or steamed dishes instead of fried ones, you can significantly reduce calorie and fat intake. Choosing salads with lean proteins like chicken, fish, or tofu provides a balanced meal rich in vitamins, minerals, and essential nutrients. Additionally, requesting dressings and sauces on the side allows you to control the amount used, preventing excess calorie consumption.

With a little mindfulness and these simple strategies, you can enjoy dining out without compromising your commitment to a healthy diet.

Eating Raw Foods is Always Better: Eating raw foods is often considered healthier, but this isn't always the case. While raw fruits and vegetables can retain more nutrients in some instances, cooking can actually enhance the bioavailability of certain nutrients, making them easier for the body to absorb. For example, cooking tomatoes increases the availability of lycopene, a powerful antioxidant, and cooking carrots enhances the absorption of beta-carotene, which is vital for eye health. A balanced approach that includes both raw and cooked foods can provide a wider range of nutrients and health benefits.

Eating Small Portions Automatically Means Healthy: Eating small portions doesn't automatically mean you're eating healthy. The quality of the food you consume matters a lot more. Small portions of nutrient-poor foods won't provide the essential vitamins and minerals your body needs. Instead, focus on eating nutrient-dense foods like fruits, vegetables, whole grains, and lean proteins in appropriate portions. In fact, eating good, nutrient-dense foods can help you feel satiated naturally, reducing the likelihood of overeating.

Eating a Vegetarian or Vegan Diet Guarantees Health: While well-planned vegetarian and vegan diets can be highly nutritious, they require careful attention to ensure adequate intake of essential nutrients like protein, iron, calcium, and vitamin B12. Without proper planning, it's easy to miss out on these crucial nutrients, leading to deficiencies that can affect overall health. To maintain a balanced and healthy diet, vegetarians and vegans need to include a variety of nutrient-dense foods, such as legumes, nuts, seeds, fortified foods, and leafy greens, and may need to consider supplements to meet their nutritional needs.

Salads are Always the Healthiest Option: Salads are often perceived as the healthiest option, but this isn't always the case. While salads can indeed be a nutritious choice, toppings like creamy dressings, fried additions, and excessive cheese can introduce unhealthy fats and extra calories, potentially negating the health benefits of the vegetables. Additionally, some pre-made salads can contain high levels of sodium and added sugars. To ensure your salad is genuinely healthy, opt for lean proteins such as grilled chicken, tofu, or beans, and include a variety of colorful vegetables like bell peppers, tomatoes, carrots, and leafy greens. Use light vinaigrettes or olive oil and vinegar for dressing to keep it lower in unhealthy fats and calories.

You Can't Eat Healthy on a Budget: Eating healthy doesn't have to be expensive. Choosing budget-friendly staples like beans, lentils, frozen fruits and vegetables, and buying in-season produce can help stretch your food dollars while maintaining a nutritious diet. Beans and lentils are excellent sources of protein and fiber, offering great nutritional value at a very low cost. Frozen fruits and vegetables are just as nutritious as their fresh counterparts and often more affordable, especially when certain items are out of season. Purchasing in-season produce not only ensures better flavor and nutrition but also helps you save money since these items are typically less expensive when they are abundant. Additionally, planning meals ahead, buying in bulk, and cooking at home can further reduce costs while allowing you to control the quality and healthiness of your meals. By making these smart choices, you can enjoy a diverse, balanced, and nutritious diet without breaking the bank.

Superfoods: Nutrient-Rich Foods for Health and Vitality

"Superfoods" is a term used to describe foods that are exceptionally nutrient-dense and believed to provide significant health benefits beyond basic nutrition. These foods are often rich in vitamins, minerals, antioxidants, and other beneficial compounds that support overall well-being and may reduce the risk of chronic diseases. While there is no official definition or list of superfoods, certain foods frequently earn this designation due to their impressive nutrient profiles and potential health-promoting properties.

Examples of superfoods include:

Berries: Blueberries, strawberries, raspberries, and other berries are rich in antioxidants such as anthocyanins and vitamin C, which help combat oxidative stress and inflammation.

Leafy Greens: Kale, spinach, Swiss chard, and other leafy greens are packed with vitamins (like vitamin K and folate), minerals (such as iron and calcium), and phytochemicals that support immune function and promote bone health.

Nuts and Seeds: Almonds, walnuts, chia seeds, and flaxseeds are high in healthy fats (omega-3 fatty acids), fiber, and protein, which can contribute to heart health and aid in weight management.

Fatty Fish: Salmon, mackerel, and sardines are rich in omega-3 fatty acids, which are essential for brain health, reducing inflammation, and supporting cardiovascular function.

Whole Grains: Quinoa, oats, brown rice, and barley are packed with fiber, vitamins, and minerals. They provide sustained energy, support digestive health, and may help reduce the risk of chronic diseases like diabetes and heart disease.

Yogurt and Fermented Foods: Yogurt, kefir, sauerkraut, and kimchi contain probiotics— beneficial bacteria that support gut health, digestion, and immune function.

Turmeric: Known for its anti-inflammatory properties, turmeric contains curcumin, a compound with potential health benefits such as reducing inflammation and improving joint health.

Green Tea: Green tea is rich in antioxidants called catechins, which may help protect against heart disease, improve brain function, and boost metabolism.

Superfoods are often promoted as part of a balanced diet to enhance overall health and well-being. Incorporating a variety of superfoods into your meals can help ensure you receive a wide range of essential nutrients and bioactive compounds that support various bodily functions and may offer protective effects against certain diseases. However, it's important to note that no single food or group of foods can provide all the nutrients your body needs, and a diverse diet that includes a variety of nutrient-dense foods is key to optimal health.

The Importance of Hydration

Hydration is crucial for your overall health and well-being, influencing nearly every bodily function. Water, making up about 60% of your body weight, plays critical roles like regulating body temperature through sweating, especially important during physical exertion or in hot environments. It also ensures your cells receive essential nutrients and oxygen for energy production, growth, and repair, while effectively removing waste products and toxins to support optimal organ function. Water's ability to lubricate joints, cushion organs, and aid digestion by facilitating nutrient absorption underscores its role in maintaining your body's biochemical processes and physiological balance.

Your hydration needs are influenced by various factors such as your level of physical activity, environmental conditions like heat and humidity, and your health status and age. Infants, children, older adults, and pregnant or breastfeeding women have specific hydration requirements due to their unique physiological needs. Dehydration occurs when your body loses more fluid than it takes in, leading to symptoms like thirst, dry mouth, dark urine, fatigue, and dizziness. Severe dehydration can result in serious conditions such as heat-related illnesses, kidney stones, and urinary tract infections.

Hydration is critical for cognitive function as well, impacting concentration, memory retention, and mood regulation. Research consistently shows that even mild dehydration can impair these cognitive abilities. When you're not adequately hydrated, your brain may receive less blood flow and oxygen, hindering its efficiency in performing tasks. Additionally, dehydration can disrupt neurotransmitter function, affecting learning, memory formation, and emotional balance. Changes in brain structure and function due to dehydration may further contribute to difficulties in decision-making, problem-solving, and emotional regulation.

Furthermore, dehydration-induced fatigue and discomfort can exacerbate cognitive decline, causing increased tiredness, irritability, and difficulty concentrating. These symptoms can significantly affect your daily activities and performance, both at work and in your personal life.

Therefore, maintaining proper hydration levels is crucial for optimizing your physical and cognitive performance, ultimately supporting your overall health, vitality, and well-being.

Choked Lifelines: How Fat Clogs Our Arteries

Imagine your arteries as pristine rivers, once flowing freely with life-giving water, nourishing every corner of your body with vitality and energy. Now, envision fat as a creeping, oily sludge slowly infiltrating these pristine waters.

Initially, this sludge appears harmless, barely noticeable, but over time, it accumulates, coating the riverbeds and narrowing the channels. What was once a swift, clear current now struggles against the encroaching sludge, slowing to a sluggish crawl.

As the sludge thickens, it forms into stubborn blockades within the river channels. Imagine rocks and debris accumulating, causing dangerous logjams that disrupt the natural flow. These blockades prevent the smooth passage of essential nutrients and oxygen to distant villages downstream — your organs and tissues — which depend on this vital flow for their survival.

The relentless accumulation of fat transforms these once-clear rivers into choked, stagnant waterways. The riverbanks harden and become rigid, losing their flexibility and ability to expand and contract with the natural ebb and flow of life. Like rivers forced into narrow, inflexible canals, your arteries become constricted and less responsive to the body's needs.

With each passing day, the burden on your cardiovascular system increases. Your heart, the tireless pump driving the flow, strains against the resistance of these clogged arteries. The risk of catastrophic blockages looms large, threatening to rupture and devastate the fragile balance of your body's natural ecosystem.

Conclusions

Throughout this journey, we've uncovered the hidden truths about our modern diet and its profound impact on our health. From the deceptive allure of junk foods to the harmful effects of sugary beverages and processed meats, each chapter has revealed how these choices can lead to obesity, diabetes, cardiovascular disease, and a host of other serious health issues. We've explored how these foods affect not only our physical health but also our mental well-being, from cognitive function to emotional stability.

Delving deeper, we've examined the intricate connection between our gut health and overall immunity, recognizing the microbiome as a hidden powerhouse that influences everything from digestion to mood regulation. We've confronted common objections and cultural norms that perpetuate unhealthy eating habits, and we've scrutinized the role of industry influence and governmental inaction in shaping our dietary landscape.

Yet, amidst these challenges, we've also explored strategies for reclaiming control over our health. From understanding the science of food addiction to embracing mindful eating and the ancient practice of fasting, we've provided tools to break free from unhealthy habits and cultivate a sustainable approach to nutrition.

Breaking free from the grip of junk food addiction is pivotal to this journey. By recognizing the addictive nature of certain foods and understanding how they manipulate our brain chemistry, we empower ourselves to make informed choices. It's about replacing empty calories with nutrient-dense foods that nourish our bodies and minds. It's about fostering a positive relationship with food that supports our long-term health goals.

As we conclude, the message is clear: adopting healthy daily habits is not only beneficial but essential for a vibrant and fulfilling life. It's about recognizing the power of nourishing foods, hydrating our bodies adequately, and nurturing our microbiome. It's about making informed choices that prioritize long-term well-being over short-term indulgence.

Now is the time to take action. Let's commit to recognizing and choosing healthy foods, fostering a supportive gut-brain connection, and embracing mindful eating practices. Together, we can overcome the challenges posed by our modern diet culture and pave the way for a healthier future. Here's to embracing a lifestyle that honors our bodies, minds, and spirits – one nourishing choice at a time.

Printed in Great Britain
by Amazon

55818369R00106